100
Best
Slow Cooker

100

Best
Slow Cooker

The ultimate guide to the slow cooker including

100 delicious recipes

This edition published in 2012
LOVE FOOD is an imprint of Parragon Books Ltd

Parragon
Queen Street House
4 Queen Street
Bath BA1 1HE, UK

www.parragon.com

ISBN: 978-1-4454-6192-2

Printed in Indonesia

Cover photography by Clive Streeter
Additional photography by Mike Cooper
Introduction by Linda Doeser

Notes for the Reader
This book uses both metric and imperial measurements. Follow the same
units of measurement throughout; do not mix metric and imperial. All
spoon measurements are level: teaspoons are assumed to be 5 ml, and
tablespoons are assumed to be 15 ml. Unless otherwise stated, milk is
assumed to be full fat, eggs and individual vegetables are medium, and
pepper is freshly ground black pepper.

The times given are an approximate guide only. Preparation times differ
according to the techniques used by different people and the cooking
times may also vary from those given. Optional ingredients, variations or
serving suggestions have not been included in the calculations.

Recipes using raw or very lightly cooked eggs should be avoided by
infants, the elderly, pregnant women, convalescents and anyone suffering
from an illness. Pregnant and breastfeeding women are advised to avoid
eating peanuts and peanut products. Sufferers from nut allergies should
be aware that some of the ready-made ingredients used in the recipes in
this book may contain nuts. Always check the packaging before use.

Vegetarians should be aware that some of the ready-prepared ingredients
used in the recipes in this book may contain animal products. Always
check the packaging before use.

CONTENTS

INTRODUCTION

A wide variety of tasty, nourishing, healthy and economical meals that are easy to prepare and don't require masses of time and effort in the kitchen – that's what all family cooks would like. But somehow it doesn't always work that way – unless, of course, you use a slow cooker.

Slow cooking has a venerable history but has been revolutionized and updated to the twenty-first century by the modern electric slow cooker. After vegetables have been sliced or chopped, onions softened and meat browned, the ingredients of a delicious one-pot dish are packed into the cooking pot, then covered with the lid and the cooker switched on. You can then go off to work, visit friends, take the children out for the day or whatever you like, safely leaving supper to bubble gently into succulent perfection ready to eat when you return.

As the slow cooker operates at a much lower temperature than the oven or hob, there's no risk of its contents boiling over or drying out and it can be safely left for up to 12 hours. It's ideal for tenderizing less expensive cuts of meat and also helps the family budget by using only about as much electricity as a light bulb. Once it has reached the optimum temperature, steam condenses on the inside of the lid, forming a seal that locks in flavour and essential vitamins and minerals, so it's both a tasty and a healthy option.

Top tips

• Read the manufacturer's instructions as models may vary.

• Stand the cooker on a flat surface out of the reach of children and make sure that the electric cable isn't dangling.

• Thaw frozen food, especially poultry, before adding it to the slow cooker.

• If your cooker has a removable cooking pot, lift this out before adding the ingredients to avoid spills and splashes in the cooker base.

• For best results the cooker should be at least half full but never more than two-thirds full.

• As root vegetables take a long time to cook, make sure that they are completely covered with liquid.

• Once the cooker has been switched on, don't open the lid, especially during the first half of the cooking time, as this will break the condensation seal and will reduce the temperature, and it will take up to 20 minutes to return to the optimum temperature.

• If leaving the cooker unattended, set the control to low. If you have an auto setting that starts on high and then automatically switches to low, you can also use this.

• Switch off the cooker before lifting out the removable cooking pot and serving.

• Don't use the slow cooker for reheating leftovers.

1

MEAT

01

Traditional Pot Roast

SERVES 6

1 onion, finely chopped

4 carrots, sliced

4 baby turnips, sliced

4 celery sticks, sliced

2 potatoes, sliced

1 sweet potato, sliced

1.3–1.8 kg/3–4 lb topside of beef, in one piece

1 bouquet garni

300 ml/10 fl oz hot beef stock

salt and pepper

Method

1 Place the onion, carrots, turnips, celery, potatoes and sweet potato in the slow cooker and stir to mix well.

2 Rub the beef all over with salt and pepper, then place on top of the bed of vegetables. Add the bouquet garni and pour in the stock. Cover and cook on low for 9–10 hours, until the beef is cooked to your liking. Serve immediately.

02

Traditional Beef Stew

SERVES 6

4 tbsp plain flour

1 kg/2 lb 4 oz braising steak, cut into 4-cm/1½-inch cubes

2 tbsp sunflower oil

85 g/3 oz bacon, diced

55 g/2 oz butter

2 onions, thinly sliced

4 carrots, sliced

600 g/1 lb 5 oz potatoes, cut into chunks

115 g/4 oz mushrooms, sliced

1 bay leaf

2 fresh thyme sprigs, finely chopped, plus extra sprigs to garnish

1 tbsp finely chopped fresh parsley

400 g/14 oz canned chopped tomatoes

350 ml/12 fl oz beef stock

salt and pepper

Method

1 Put the flour into a plastic food bag and season to taste with salt and pepper. Add the steak cubes, in batches, hold the top securely and shake well to coat. Transfer the meat to a plate.

2 Heat the oil in a large frying pan. Add the bacon and cook over a low heat, stirring frequently, for 5 minutes. Add the steak cubes, increase the heat to medium and cook, stirring frequently, for 8–10 minutes, until evenly browned. Remove the meat with a slotted spoon and set aside on a plate.

3 Wipe out the pan with kitchen paper, then return to a low heat and melt the butter. Add the onions and cook, stirring occasionally, for 5 minutes, until softened. Add the carrots, potatoes and mushrooms and cook, stirring occasionally, for a further 5 minutes.

4 Season to taste with salt and pepper, add the bay leaf, chopped thyme, parsley and tomatoes and pour in the stock. Bring to the boil, stirring occasionally, then remove the pan from the heat and transfer the mixture to the slow cooker. Stir in the meat, cover and cook on low for 8–9 hours. Remove and discard the bay leaf. Garnish with thyme sprigs and serve immediately.

03

Beef in Beer

SERVES 4–6

4 tbsp sunflower oil

1 kg/2 lb 4 oz topside of beef,
    in one piece

1.5 kg/3 lb 5 oz red onions,
    thinly sliced

500 ml/18 fl oz beef stock

1½ tbsp plain flour

350 ml/12 fl oz beer

3 garlic cloves, chopped

1 strip thinly pared
    lemon rind

1 bay leaf

2 tbsp molasses

salt and pepper

fresh flat-leaf parsley sprigs,
    to garnish

Method

1 Heat the oil in a large frying pan. Add the beef and cook over a medium–high heat, turning occasionally, for 5–8 minutes, until evenly browned. Transfer the beef to the slow cooker.

2 Reduce the heat to low and add the onions to the pan. Cook, stirring occasionally, for 5 minutes, until softened. Stir in 2 tablespoons of the stock, scraping up the sediment from the base of the pan, and cook until all the liquid has evaporated. Add another 2 tablespoons of the stock and continue to cook for a further 15 minutes, adding 2 tablespoons of the stock each time the previous addition has evaporated.

3 Stir in the flour and cook, stirring constantly, for 1 minute, then gradually stir in the remaining stock and the beer. Increase the heat to medium and bring to the boil, stirring constantly.

4 Stir in the garlic, lemon rind, bay leaf and molasses and season to taste with salt and pepper. Transfer the onion mixture to the slow cooker, cover and cook on low for 8–9 hours, until the beef is cooked to your liking. Serve immediately, garnished with parsley sprigs.

04

Pot Roast with Beer

SERVES 4–6

2 small onions, each cut into
    8 wedges

8 small carrots, halved lengthways

1 fennel bulb, cut into 8 wedges

2.25 kg/5 lb rolled chuck steak

2 tbsp Dijon mustard

1 tbsp plain flour

100 ml/3 1/2 fl oz beer

salt and pepper

Method

1 Place the onions, carrots and fennel in the slow cooker and season to taste with salt and pepper. Place the beef on top.

2 Mix the mustard and flour together to form a paste and spread it over the beef. Season well and pour over the beer. Cover and cook on low for 8 hours.

3 Remove the beef and vegetables with a slotted spoon and transfer to a warmed serving platter. Skim the excess fat from the juices and pour the juices into a jug to serve with the beef. Serve immediately.

05

Hungarian Goulash

SERVES 4

4 tbsp sunflower oil

650 g/1 lb 7 oz braising steak,
   cut into 2.5-cm/1-inch cubes

2 tsp plain flour

2 tsp paprika

300 ml/10 fl oz beef stock

3 onions, chopped

4 carrots, diced

1 large potato or 2 medium
   potatoes, diced

1 bay leaf

1/2–1 tsp caraway seeds

400 g/14 oz canned chopped
   tomatoes

2 tbsp soured cream

salt and pepper

Method

1 Heat half the oil in a heavy-based frying pan. Add the beef and cook over a medium heat, stirring frequently, until evenly browned. Reduce the heat and stir in the flour and paprika. Cook, stirring constantly, for 2 minutes. Gradually stir in the stock and bring to the boil, then transfer the mixture to the slow cooker.

2 Wipe out the pan with kitchen paper, then heat the remaining oil. Add the onions and cook over a low heat, stirring occasionally, for 5 minutes, until softened. Stir in the carrots and potato and cook for a further few minutes. Add the bay leaf, caraway seeds and tomatoes. Season to taste with salt and pepper.

3 Transfer the vegetable mixture to the slow cooker and stir well, then cover and cook on low for 9 hours, until the meat is tender.

4 Remove and discard the bay leaf. Stir in the soured cream and transfer to warmed serving plates. Serve immediately.

06

Beef Bourguignon

SERVES 6

2 tbsp plain flour

900 g/2 lb braising steak, trimmed
and cut into 2.5-cm/1-inch cubes

6 rashers streaky bacon, derinded
and chopped

3 tbsp olive oil

25 g/1 oz unsalted butter

12 baby onions or shallots

2 garlic cloves, finely chopped

150 ml/5 fl oz beef stock

450 ml/16 fl oz full-bodied red wine

1 bouquet garni

140 g/5 oz mushrooms, quartered

salt and pepper

Method

1 Put the flour into a plastic food bag and season to taste with
salt and pepper. Add the steak cubes, in batches, hold the top
securely and shake well to coat. Transfer the meat to a plate.

2 Cook the bacon in a large heavy-based saucepan, stirring
occasionally, until the fat runs and the bacon is crisp. Using a
slotted spoon, transfer the bacon to a plate. Add the oil to the
saucepan. When it is hot, add the steak cubes and cook, in batches,
stirring occasionally, for 5 minutes, until evenly browned. Transfer
to the plate with a slotted spoon.

3 Add the butter to the saucepan. When it has melted, add the
onions and garlic and cook, stirring occasionally, for 5 minutes.
Return the bacon and steak to the pan and pour in the stock and
wine. Bring to the boil.

4 Transfer the mixture to the slow cooker and add the bouquet
garni. Cover and cook on low for 7 hours, until the meat is tender.

5 Add the mushrooms to the slow cooker and stir well. Re-cover
and cook on high for 15 minutes.

6 Remove and discard the bouquet garni. Taste and adjust the
seasoning, adding salt and pepper if needed. Transfer to warmed
serving bowls and serve immediately.

07

Beef Ragù with Tagliatelle

SERVES 6

3 tbsp olive oil

85 g/3 oz pancetta or bacon, diced

1 onion, chopped

1 garlic clove, finely chopped

1 carrot, chopped

1 celery stick, chopped

450 g/1 lb minced steak

125 ml/4 fl oz red wine

2 tbsp tomato purée

400 g/14 oz canned chopped tomatoes

300 ml/10 fl oz beef stock

1/2 tsp dried oregano

1 bay leaf

450 g/1 lb dried tagliatelle

salt and pepper

grated Parmesan cheese, to serve

Method

1 Heat the oil in a saucepan. Add the pancetta and cook over a medium heat, stirring frequently, for 3 minutes. Reduce the heat, add the onion, garlic, carrot and celery and cook, stirring occasionally, for 5 minutes, until the vegetables have softened.

2 Increase the heat to medium and add the minced steak. Cook, stirring frequently and breaking it up with a wooden spoon, for 8–10 minutes, until evenly browned. Pour in the wine and cook for a few minutes, until the alcohol has evaporated, then stir in the tomato purée, tomatoes, stock, oregano and bay leaf and season to taste with salt and pepper.

3 Bring to the boil, then transfer the ragù to the slow cooker. Cover and cook on low for 8–8 1/2 hours.

4 Shortly before serving, bring a large saucepan of lightly salted water to the boil. Add the pasta, bring back to the boil and cook for 8–10 minutes, until tender but still firm to the bite. Drain and tip into a warmed serving bowl. Remove and discard the bay leaf, then add the ragù to the pasta. Toss with two forks, sprinkle with the Parmesan and serve immediately.

08

Beef & Chipotle Burritos

SERVES 4

1 tbsp olive oil

1 onion, sliced

600 g/1 lb 5 oz beef chuck steak

1 dried chipotle pepper, soaked in boiling water for 20 minutes

1 garlic clove, crushed

1 tsp ground cumin

400 g/14 oz canned chopped tomatoes

8 tortillas

salt and pepper

soured cream and green salad, to serve

Method

1 Heat the oil in a pan and fry the onion for 3–4 minutes until golden. Tip into the slow cooker and arrange the beef on top. Drain and chop the chipotle. Sprinkle over the meat with the garlic, cumin, tomatoes, salt and pepper.

2 Cover and cook on low for 4 hours, until the meat is tender.

3 Warm the tortillas. Remove the beef and shred with a fork. Divide between the tortillas and spoon over the sauce. Wrap, and serve with soured cream and green salad.

09

Chunky Beef Chilli

SERVES 4

250 g/9 oz dried red kidney beans,
  soaked overnight

600 ml/1 pint cold water

2 garlic cloves, chopped

5 tbsp tomato purée

1 small green chilli, chopped

2 tsp ground cumin

2 tsp ground coriander

600 g/1 lb 5 oz chuck steak, diced

1 large onion, chopped

1 large green pepper, deseeded
  and sliced

salt and pepper

soured cream, to serve

Method

1 Drain the beans and place in a saucepan, cover with cold water and bring to the boil. Boil rapidly for 10 minutes, then remove from the heat and drain. Place the beans in the slow cooker and add 600 ml cold water.

2 Mix the garlic, tomato purée, chilli, cumin and coriander together in a large bowl. Add the steak, onion and green pepper and mix to coat evenly.

3 Place the meat and vegetables on top of the beans, cover and cook on low for 9 hours, until the beans and meat are tender. Stir and season to taste with salt and pepper.

4 Transfer to warmed serving bowls and top with a swirl of soured cream. Serve immediately.

10

Neapolitan Beef

SERVES 6

300 ml/10 fl oz red wine

4 tbsp olive oil

1 celery stick, chopped

2 shallots, sliced

4 garlic cloves, finely chopped

1 bay leaf

10 fresh basil leaves, plus extra
  to garnish

3 fresh parsley sprigs

pinch of grated nutmeg

pinch of ground cinnamon

2 cloves

1.5 kg/3 lb 5 oz beef silverside, in
  one piece

1–2 garlic cloves, thinly sliced

55 g/2 oz streaky bacon or pancetta,
  derinded and chopped

400 g/14 oz canned chopped
  tomatoes

2 tbsp tomato purée

Method

1 Combine the wine, half the oil, the celery, shallots, garlic, herbs and spices in a large non-metallic bowl. Add the beef, cover and leave to marinate, turning occasionally, for 12 hours.

2 Drain the beef, reserving the marinade, and pat dry with kitchen paper. Make small incisions all over the beef using a sharp knife. Insert a slice of garlic and a piece of bacon in each 'pocket'. Heat the remaining oil in a large frying pan. Add the meat and cook over a medium heat, turning frequently, until evenly browned. Transfer to the slow cooker.

3 Strain the reserved marinade into the frying pan and bring to the boil. Stir in the tomatoes and tomato purée. Stir well, then pour the mixture over the beef. Cover and cook on low for about 8–9 hours, until the beef is cooked to your liking. If possible, turn the beef over halfway through the cooking time.

4 Remove the beef from the slow cooker and place on a carving board. Cover with foil and leave to stand for 10–15 minutes to firm up. Cut into slices and transfer to a platter. Spoon over the sauce, garnish with basil leaves and serve immediately.

11

Caribbean Beef Stew

SERVES 6

450 g/1 lb braising steak

450 g/1 lb diced pumpkin or other squash

1 onion, chopped

1 red pepper, deseeded and chopped

2 garlic cloves, finely chopped

2.5-cm/1-inch piece fresh ginger, finely chopped

1 tbsp sweet or hot paprika

225 ml/8 fl oz beef stock

400 g/14 oz canned chopped tomatoes

400 g/14 oz canned pigeon peas or chickpeas, drained and rinsed

400 g/14 oz canned black-eyed beans, drained and rinsed

salt and pepper

Method

1 Trim off any visible fat from the steak, then dice the meat. Heat a large heavy-based saucepan without adding any extra fat. Add the meat and cook, stirring constantly, for a few minutes, until evenly browned. Stir in the pumpkin, onion and red pepper and cook for 1 minute, then add the garlic, ginger and paprika. Pour in the stock and tomatoes and bring to the boil.

2 Transfer the mixture to the slow cooker, cover and cook on low for 7 hours. Add the pigeon peas and black-eyed beans to the stew and season to taste with salt and pepper. Re-cover and cook on high for 30 minutes. Transfer to warmed serving bowls and serve immediately.

12

Beef in Coffee Sauce

SERVES 6

4 tbsp sunflower oil

1.3 kg/3 lb braising steak,
    cut into 2.5-cm/1-inch cubes

4 onions, sliced

1 garlic clove, finely chopped

5 tbsp plain flour

300 ml/10 fl oz red wine

pinch of dried oregano

1 small fresh rosemary sprig

500 ml/18 fl oz black coffee

salt and pepper

fresh marjoram sprigs, to garnish

mashed sweet potatoes, to serve

Method

1 Heat the oil in a large frying pan. Add the steak cubes and cook over a medium heat, stirring frequently, for 8–10 minutes, until evenly browned. Transfer to the slow cooker with a slotted spoon.

2 Add the onions and garlic to the pan, reduce the heat and cook, stirring occasionally, for 10 minutes, until softened and just beginning to colour. Stir in the flour and cook, stirring constantly, for 1 minute. Gradually stir in the wine, a little at a time. Add the oregano and rosemary, season to taste with salt and pepper, pour in the coffee and bring to the boil, stirring constantly.

3 Transfer the mixture to the slow cooker. Cover and cook on low for 8–9 hours, until the meat is tender. Remove and discard the rosemary sprig. Taste and adjust the seasoning, adding salt and pepper if needed. Transfer to warmed serving plates, garnish with marjoram sprigs and serve immediately with mashed sweet potatoes.

13

Venison Casserole

SERVES 6

3 tbsp olive oil

1 kg/2 lb 4 oz braising venison, cut
  into 3-cm/1¼-inch cubes

2 onions, thinly sliced

2 garlic cloves, chopped

350 ml/12 fl oz beef stock

2 tbsp plain flour

125 ml/4 fl oz port

2 tbsp redcurrant jelly

6 juniper berries, crushed

4 cloves, crushed

pinch of ground cinnamon

pinch of freshly grated nutmeg

salt and pepper

chopped fresh flat-leaf parsley,
  to garnish

mashed potatoes, to serve

Method

1 Heat the oil in a heavy-based frying pan. Add the venison and cook over a high heat, stirring frequently, for 5 minutes, until browned all over. Using a slotted spoon, transfer the meat to the slow cooker.

2 Add the onions and garlic to the frying pan, reduce the heat and cook, stirring occasionally, for 5 minutes, until softened. Transfer them to the slow cooker.

3 Gradually stir the stock into the frying pan, scraping up any sediment from the base, then bring to the boil, stirring constantly. Sprinkle the flour over the meat in the slow cooker and stir well to coat evenly. Stir in the hot stock, then stir in the port, redcurrant jelly, juniper berries, cloves, cinnamon and nutmeg. Season to taste with salt and pepper. Cover and cook on low for 7–8 hours, until the meat is tender.

4 Taste and adjust the seasoning, adding salt and pepper if needed. Remove and discard the cloves. Garnish with parsley and serve immediately with mashed potatoes.

14

Lamb with Spring Vegetables

SERVES 4–6

5 tbsp olive oil

6 shallots, chopped

1 garlic clove, chopped

2 celery sticks, chopped

2 tbsp plain flour

700 g/1 lb 9 oz boned leg or
  shoulder of lamb, cut into
  2.5-cm/1-inch cubes

850 ml/1½ pints chicken stock

115 g/4 oz pearl barley, rinsed

225 g/8 oz small turnips, halved

225 g/8 oz baby carrots

225 g/8 oz frozen petits pois, thawed

225 g/8 oz frozen baby broad beans,
  thawed

salt and pepper

chopped fresh parsley, to garnish

Method

1 Heat 3 tablespoons of the oil in a flameproof casserole or large saucepan. Add the shallots, garlic and celery and cook over a low heat, stirring occasionally, for 8–10 minutes, until softened and lightly browned.

2 Meanwhile, put the flour into a plastic food bag and season well with salt and pepper. Add the lamb cubes, in batches, hold the top securely and shake well to coat. Transfer the meat to a plate.

3 Using a slotted spoon, transfer the softened vegetables to the slow cooker. Add the remaining oil to the pan and heat. Add the lamb, in batches if necessary, increase the heat to medium and cook, stirring frequently, for 8–10 minutes, until evenly browned.

4 Return all the lamb to the pan. Gradually stir in the stock, scraping up the sediment from the base of the pan. Stir in the pearl barley, turnips and carrots, season to taste with salt and pepper and bring to the boil. Transfer the mixture to the slow cooker and stir well. Cover and cook on low for 8–10 hours, until the lamb is tender.

5 Add the petits pois and broad beans to the slow cooker, sprinkling them evenly on top of the stew. Re-cover and cook on low for a further 30 minutes, until heated through. Stir well, then taste and adjust the seasoning, adding salt and pepper if needed. Garnish with parsley and serve immediately.

15

Daube of Lamb

SERVES 6

300 ml/10 fl oz dry white wine

3 tbsp brandy

1 tbsp olive oil

1 fresh rosemary sprig

1 bay leaf

1 tbsp chopped fresh parsley

2 cloves

6 allspice berries

6 black peppercorns

1 strip thinly pared orange rind

4 shallots, sliced

2 carrots, sliced

2 garlic cloves, finely chopped

1.3 kg/3 lb diced lamb

115 g/4 oz plain flour

4 rashers bacon, cut into
2.5-cm/1-inch strips

2 onions, chopped

500 ml/18 fl oz beef stock

salt and pepper

crusty bread, to serve

Method

1 Put the wine, brandy, oil, rosemary, bay leaf, parsley, cloves, allspice berries, peppercorns, orange rind, shallots, carrots, garlic and lamb into a large non-metallic bowl and mix well. Cover with clingfilm and leave to marinate overnight in the refrigerator.

2 Drain the lamb cubes, reserving the marinade. Pat the lamb dry with kitchen paper. Put the flour into a plastic food bag and season to taste with salt and pepper. Add the lamb cubes, in batches, hold the top securely and shake well to coat. Transfer the meat to a plate.

3 Cook the bacon in a large non-stick or heavy-based saucepan over a medium heat for 3 minutes. Add the onions, reduce the heat and cook, stirring occasionally, for 5 minutes, until softened. Add the lamb, increase the heat to medium and cook, stirring frequently, for 8–10 minutes, until evenly browned. Pour in the reserved marinade and the stock and bring to the boil, stirring occasionally.

4 Transfer the mixture to the slow cooker, cover and cook on low for 8–9 hours, until the meat is tender. Skim off any fat from the surface and remove and discard the rosemary, bay leaf and orange rind. Taste and adjust the seasoning if necessary. Transfer to warmed serving plates and serve immediately with crusty bread.

16

Lamb Tagine

SERVES 6

3 tbsp olive oil

2 red onions, chopped

2 garlic cloves, finely chopped

2.5-cm/1-inch piece fresh ginger, finely chopped

1 yellow pepper, deseeded and chopped

1 kg/2 lb 4 oz boneless shoulder of lamb, trimmed and cut into 2.5-cm/1-inch cubes

850 ml/1 1/2 pints lamb or chicken stock

225 g/8 oz ready-to-eat dried apricots, halved

1 tbsp clear honey

4 tbsp lemon juice

pinch of saffron threads

5-cm/2-inch cinnamon stick

salt and pepper

toasted flaked almonds and fresh coriander sprigs, to garnish

Method

1 Heat the oil in a large heavy-based saucepan. Add the onions, garlic, ginger and yellow pepper and cook over a low heat, stirring occasionally, for 5 minutes, until the onion has softened. Add the lamb and stir well to mix, then pour in the stock. Add the apricots, honey, lemon juice, saffron and cinnamon stick and season to taste with salt and pepper. Bring to the boil.

2 Transfer the mixture to the slow cooker. Cover and cook on low for 8 1/2 hours, until the meat is tender.

3 Remove and discard the cinnamon stick. Transfer to warmed serving bowls and garnish with flaked almonds and coriander sprigs. Serve immediately.

17

Lamb Shanks with Olives

SERVES 4

1½ tbsp plain flour

4 lamb shanks

2 tbsp olive oil

1 onion, sliced

2 garlic cloves, finely chopped

2 tsp sweet paprika

400 g/14 oz canned chopped
    tomatoes

2 tbsp tomato purée

2 carrots, sliced

2 tsp sugar

225 ml/8 fl oz red wine

5-cm/2-inch cinnamon stick

2 fresh rosemary sprigs

115 g/4 oz stoned black olives

2 tbsp lemon juice

2 tbsp chopped fresh mint,
    plus extra leaves to garnish

salt and pepper

Method

1 Put the flour into a plastic food bag and season to taste
with salt and pepper. Add the lamb shanks, hold the top
securely and shake well to coat.

2 Heat the oil in a large heavy-based saucepan. Add the
lamb shanks and cook over a medium heat, turning frequently,
for 6–8 minutes, until evenly browned. Transfer to a plate and
set aside.

3 Add the onion and garlic to the saucepan and cook, stirring
frequently, for 5 minutes, until softened. Stir in the paprika
and cook for 1 minute. Add the tomatoes, tomato purée,
carrots, sugar, wine, cinnamon stick and rosemary and bring to
the boil.

4 Transfer the mixture to the slow cooker and add the lamb
shanks. Cover and cook on low for 8 hours, until the lamb is
very tender.

5 Add the olives, lemon juice and chopped mint to the slow
cooker. Re-cover and cook on high for 30 minutes. Remove and
discard the rosemary and cinnamon stick. Transfer to warmed
serving plates, garnish with mint leaves and serve immediately.

18

Cured Ham Cooked in Cider

SERVES 6

1 kg/2 lb 4 oz boneless gammon
   joint

1 onion, halved

4 cloves

6 black peppercorns

1 tsp juniper berries

1 celery stick, chopped

1 carrot, sliced

1 litre/1¾ pints medium cider

fresh salad, to serve

Method

1 Place a trivet or rack in the slow cooker, if you like, and stand the gammon on it. Otherwise, just place the gammon in the slow cooker. Stud each onion half with two of the cloves and add to the slow cooker with the peppercorns, juniper berries, celery and carrot.

2 Pour in the cider, cover and cook on low for 8 hours, until the meat is tender.

3 Remove the gammon from the cooker and place on a board. Tent with foil and leave to stand for 10–15 minutes. Discard the cooking liquid and flavourings.

4 Cut off any rind and fat from the gammon joint and carve into slices. Transfer to serving plates and serve immediately with a fresh salad.

19

Pork with Apple & Herbs

SERVES 6

2 tbsp plain flour

800 g/1 lb 12 oz boneless pork,
   cut into 2.5-cm/1-inch cubes

5 tbsp sunflower oil

1 large onion, chopped

2 garlic cloves, finely chopped

2 eating apples, cored and
   cut into wedges

300 ml/10 fl oz dry cider or
   apple juice

600 ml/1 pint chicken stock

2 bay leaves

2 fresh sage sprigs

1 fresh rosemary sprig

3 tbsp chopped fresh parsley

salt and pepper

mashed potatoes, to serve

Method

1 Put the flour into a plastic food bag and season to taste with salt and pepper. Add the pork cubes, in batches, hold the top securely and shake well to coat. Transfer the meat to a plate.

2 Heat 3 tablespoons of the oil in a large frying pan. Add the pork cubes, in batches if necessary, and cook over a medium heat, stirring frequently, for 5–8 minutes, until evenly browned. Transfer to a plate and set aside.

3 Add the remaining oil to the pan and heat. Add the onion and garlic and cook over a low heat, stirring occasionally, for 10 minutes, until softened and lightly browned. Add the apple wedges and cook, stirring occasionally, for 3–5 minutes, until beginning to colour. Gradually stir in the cider and stock, scraping up any sediment from the base of the pan, and bring to the boil. Season to taste with salt and pepper, add the bay leaves, sage and rosemary and transfer to the slow cooker. Stir in the pork, cover and cook on low for 6–7 hours.

4 Remove and discard the bay leaves and the sage and rosemary sprigs. Transfer the stew to warmed individual plates and sprinkle with the parsley. Serve immediately with mashed potatoes.

20

Pork with Peppers

SERVES 4

2 tbsp olive oil

4 pork chops, trimmed of excess fat

1 shallot, chopped

2 garlic cloves, finely chopped

2 orange peppers, deseeded and sliced

1 tbsp plain flour

600 ml/1 pint chicken stock

1 tbsp medium–hot Indian curry paste

115 g/4 oz ready-to-eat dried apricots

salt and pepper

baby spinach leaves and cooked couscous, to serve

Method

1 Heat the oil in a large frying pan. Add the chops and cook over a medium heat for 2–4 minutes on each side, until evenly browned. Remove with tongs and put them into the slow cooker.

2 Add the shallot, garlic and peppers to the pan, reduce the heat and cook, stirring occasionally, for 5 minutes, until softened. Stir in the flour and cook, stirring constantly, for 1 minute. Gradually stir in the stock, a little at a time, then add the curry paste and apricots. Bring to the boil, stirring occasionally.

3 Season to taste with salt and pepper and transfer the mixture to the slow cooker. Cover and cook on low for 8–9 hours, until the meat is tender. Transfer to warmed serving plates and serve immediately with baby spinach and couscous.

21

Pork & Beans

SERVES 4

2 tbsp sunflower oil

4 pork chops, trimmed of excess fat

1 onion, chopped

400 g/14 oz canned chopped
  tomatoes

425 g/15 oz canned baked beans

butter, for greasing, plus extra
  for browning (optional)

700 g/1 lb 9 oz potatoes,
  thinly sliced

425 ml/15 fl oz hot chicken stock

salt and pepper

Method

1 Heat the oil in a frying pan. Season the chops well with salt
and pepper, add to the pan and cook over a medium heat for
2–3 minutes on each side, until evenly browned. Remove the pan
from the heat and transfer the chops to a plate.

2 Mix together the onion, tomatoes and beans in a bowl and
season to taste with salt and pepper.

3 Lightly grease the slow cooker pot with butter, then make a
layer of half the potatoes in the base. Cover with half the tomato
and bean mixture. Put the chops on top, then add the remaining
tomato and bean mixture. Cover with the remaining potato slices.

4 Pour in the stock, cover and cook on low for 8–10 hours. If
wished, remove the lid, dot the topping with butter and place the
slow cooker pot under a preheated grill to brown the potatoes
before serving.

22

Spicy Pulled Pork

SERVES 4

2 onions, sliced

1.5 kg/3 lb 5 oz boned and rolled
   pork shoulder

2 tbsp demerara sugar

2 tbsp Worcestershire sauce

1 tbsp American mustard

2 tbsp tomato ketchup

1 tbsp cider vinegar

salt and pepper

hamburger buns or ciabatta rolls,
   to serve

Method

1 Put the onions in the slow cooker and place the pork on top.
Mix the sugar, Worcestershire sauce, mustard, ketchup and vinegar
together and spread all over the surface of the pork. Season to
taste with salt and pepper. Cover and cook on low for 8 hours.

2 Remove the pork from the slow cooker and use two forks to
pull it apart into shreds.

3 Skim any excess fat from the juices and stir a little juice into
the pork. Serve in hamburger buns, with the remaining juices
for spooning over.

23

Mexican Pork Chops

SERVES 4

4 pork chops, trimmed of excess fat

2 tbsp corn oil

450 g/1 lb canned pineapple chunks
  in juice

1 red pepper, deseeded and finely
  chopped

2 fresh jalapeño chillies, deseeded
  and finely chopped

1 onion, finely chopped

1 tbsp chopped fresh coriander,
  plus extra sprigs to garnish

125 ml/4 fl oz hot chicken stock

salt and pepper

flour tortillas, to serve

Method

1 Season the chops with salt and pepper to taste. Heat the oil in a large heavy-based frying pan. Add the chops and cook over a medium heat for 2–3 minutes each side, until lightly browned. Transfer them to the slow cooker. Drain the pineapple, reserving the juice, and set aside.

2 Add the red pepper, chillies and onion to the frying pan and cook, stirring occasionally, for 5 minutes, until the onion is softened. Transfer the mixture to the slow cooker and add the chopped coriander, stock and 125 ml/4 fl oz of the reserved pineapple juice. Cover and cook on low for 6 hours, until the chops are tender.

3 Add the reserved pineapple to the slow cooker, re-cover and cook on high for 15 minutes. Garnish with coriander sprigs and serve immediately with flour tortillas.

24

Maple-Glazed Pork Ribs

SERVES 4

1 onion, finely chopped

2 plum tomatoes, diced

3 tbsp maple syrup

2 tbsp soy sauce

2 tsp hot chilli sauce

1.5 kg/3 lb 5 oz meaty pork ribs,
   cut into single ribs

salt and pepper

Method

1 Combine the onion, tomatoes, maple syrup, soy sauce, chilli sauce, and salt and pepper to taste in a large bowl. Add the pork ribs and turn to coat evenly.

2 Arrange the ribs in the slow cooker, cover and cook on high for 4 hours. If possible, turn the ribs halfway through the cooking time.

3 Lift out the ribs and place on a warmed platter. Skim the excess fat from the juices and spoon the juices over the ribs to serve.

25

Sausage & Bean Cassoulet

SERVES 4

2 tbsp sunflower oil

2 onions, chopped

2 garlic cloves, finely chopped

115 g/4 oz streaky bacon, derinded
    and chopped

500 g/1 lb 2 oz pork sausages

400 g/14 oz canned haricot, red
    kidney or black-eyed beans,
    drained and rinsed

2 tbsp chopped fresh parsley

150 ml/5 fl oz hot beef stock

4 slices French bread

55 g/2 oz Gruyère cheese, grated

Method

1 Heat the oil in a heavy-based frying pan. Add the onions and cook over a low heat, stirring occasionally, for 5 minutes, until softened. Add the garlic, bacon and sausages and cook, stirring and turning the sausages occasionally, for a further 5 minutes.

2 Using a slotted spoon, transfer the mixture from the frying pan to the slow cooker. Add the beans, parsley and stock, then cover and cook on low for 6 hours.

3 Shortly before serving, preheat the grill. Place the bread slices on the grill rack and lightly toast on one side under the preheated grill. Turn the slices over, sprinkle with the grated cheese and place under the grill until just melted.

4 Serve the cassoulet and the bread slices immediately.

POULTRY

2

26

Chicken Noodle Soup

SERVES 4

1 onion, diced

2 celery sticks, diced

2 carrots, diced

1 kg/2 lb 4 oz oven-ready chicken

700 ml/1½ pints hot chicken stock

115 g/4 oz dried egg tagliatelle

salt and pepper

2 tbsp chopped fresh dill, plus extra to garnish

Method

1 Place the onion, celery and carrots in the slow cooker. Season the chicken all over with salt and pepper and place on top. Pour the stock over. Cover and cook on low for 5 hours.

2 Leaving the juices in the slow cooker, carefully lift out the chicken and remove the meat from the carcass, discarding the bones and skin. Cut the meat into bite-sized pieces.

3 Skim the excess fat from the juices, then return the chicken to the slow cooker. Turn the setting to high.

4 Bring a large saucepan of lightly salted water to the boil. Add the tagliatelle, return to the boil and cook for 5 minutes. Drain well.

5 Stir the tagliatelle and dill into the pot, cover and cook on high for a further 20 minutes. Garnish with extra dill and serve immediately.

27

Cock-a-Leekie Soup

SERVES 6–8

12 prunes, stoned, or 12 ready-to-eat prunes

4 chicken portions

450 g/1 lb leeks, sliced

1.4 litres/2½ pints hot chicken or beef stock

1 bouquet garni

salt and pepper

Method

1 If using ordinary prunes, place them in a bowl and add cold water to cover. Set aside to soak while the soup is cooking.

2 Place the chicken portions and leeks in the slow cooker. Pour in the stock and add the bouquet garni. Cover and cook on low for 7 hours.

3 If you are going to serve the chicken in the soup, remove it from the cooker with a slotted spoon and cut the meat off the bones. Cut the meat into bite-sized pieces and return it to the cooker. Otherwise, leave the chicken portions in the slow cooker.

4 Drain the prunes, if necessary. Add the prunes to the soup and season to taste with salt and pepper. Re-cover and cook on high for 30 minutes.

5 Remove and discard the bouquet garni. Ladle the soup into warm bowls and serve immediately.

28

Chicken & Dumplings

SERVES 4

2 tbsp olive oil

1 large onion, thinly sliced

2 carrots, cut into 2-cm/
3/4-inch chunks

225 g/8 oz French beans, cut into
2.5-cm/1-inch lengths

4 skinless, boneless chicken breasts

300 ml/10 fl oz hot chicken stock

salt and pepper

Dumplings

200 g/7 oz self-raising flour

100 g/3 1/2 oz shredded suet

4 tbsp chopped parsley

Method

1 Heat 1 tablespoon of oil in a frying pan, add the onion and fry over a high heat for 3–4 minutes, or until golden. Place in the slow cooker with the carrots and beans.

2 Add the remaining oil to the pan, then add the chicken breasts and fry until golden, turning once. Arrange on top of the vegetables in a single layer, season well with salt and pepper and pour over the stock. Cover and cook on low for 4 hours.

3 Turn the slow cooker up to high while making the dumplings. Sift the flour into a bowl and stir in the suet and parsley and season to taste with salt and pepper. Stir in just enough cold water to make a fairly firm dough, mixing lightly. Divide into 12 and shape into small balls.

4 Arrange the dumplings on top of the chicken, cover and cook for 30 minutes on high. Transfer to warmed serving plates and serve immediately.

29

Chicken & Apple Pot

SERVES 4

1 tbsp olive oil

4 chicken portions,
about 175 g/6 oz each

1 onion, chopped

2 celery sticks, roughly chopped

1½ tbsp plain flour

300 ml/10 fl oz clear apple juice

150 ml/5 fl oz chicken stock

1 cooking apple, cored and
cut into quarters

2 bay leaves

1–2 tsp clear honey

1 yellow pepper, deseeded and cut
into chunks

salt and pepper

To garnish

1 large or 2 medium eating apples,
cored and sliced

1 tbsp melted butter

2 tbsp demerara sugar

1 tbsp chopped fresh mint

Method

1 Heat the oil in a heavy-based frying pan. Add the chicken and cook over a medium–high heat, turning frequently, for 10 minutes, until golden brown. Transfer to the slow cooker. Add the onion and celery to the pan and cook over a low heat for 5 minutes, until softened. Sprinkle in the flour and cook for 2 minutes, then remove the pan from the heat.

2 Gradually stir in the apple juice and stock, then return the pan to the heat and bring to the boil. Stir in the cooking apple, bay leaves and honey and season to taste. Pour the mixture over the chicken in the slow cooker, cover and cook on low for 6½ hours, until the chicken is tender and cooked through. Stir in the pepper, re-cover and cook on high for 45 minutes.

3 Shortly before serving, preheat the grill. Brush one side of the eating apple slices with half the melted butter and sprinkle with half the sugar. Cook under the preheated grill for 2–3 minutes, until the sugar has caramelized. Turn the slices over with tongs, brush with the remaining butter and sprinkle with the remaining sugar. Grill for a further 2 minutes. Transfer the stew to warmed plates and garnish with the caramelized apple slices and the mint. Serve immediately.

30

Chipotle Chicken Stew

SERVES 4–6

200 g/7 oz dried haricot beans, soaked overnight

1 large onion, sliced

1 dried chipotle pepper, soaked for 20 minutes, then drained and finely chopped

1.5 kg/3 lb 5 oz oven-ready chicken

200 ml/7 fl oz hot chicken stock

400 g/14 oz canned chopped tomatoes

1 tsp ground cumin

salt and pepper

Method

1 Drain the beans and place in a saucepan, cover with cold water and bring to the boil. Boil rapidly for 10 minutes, then remove from the heat and drain.

2 Transfer the beans to the slow cooker and add the onion and chipotle pepper. Place the chicken on top, pour over the stock and tomatoes with their can juices, sprinkle with cumin and season to taste with salt and pepper.

3 Cover and cook for 4 hours on high. Carefully remove the chicken and cut into eight pieces. Skim the excess fat from the juices and adjust the seasoning.

4 Spoon the beans into a warmed serving dish, top with the chicken and spoon the juices over. Serve immediately.

31

Chicken & Mushroom Stew

SERVES 4

15 g/½ oz unsalted butter

2 tbsp olive oil

1.8 kg/4 lb skinless chicken portions

2 red onions, sliced

2 garlic cloves, finely chopped

400 g/14 oz canned chopped
  tomatoes

2 tbsp chopped fresh flat-leaf
  parsley

6 fresh basil leaves, torn

1 tbsp sun-dried tomato purée

150 ml/5 fl oz red wine

225 g/8 oz mushrooms, sliced

salt and pepper

Method

1 Heat the butter and oil in a heavy-based frying pan. Add the chicken, in batches if necessary, and cook over a medium–high heat, turning frequently, for 10 minutes, until golden brown all over. Using a slotted spoon, transfer the chicken to the slow cooker.

2 Add the onions and garlic to the frying pan and cook over a low heat, stirring occasionally, for 10 minutes, until golden. Add the tomatoes with their can juices, stir in the parsley, basil, tomato purée and wine and season with salt and pepper. Bring to the boil, then pour the mixture over the chicken.

3 Cover the slow cooker and cook on low for 6½ hours. Stir in the mushrooms, re-cover and cook on high for 30 minutes, until the chicken is tender and the vegetables are cooked through. Taste and adjust the seasoning if necessary and serve.

32

Chicken in Riesling

SERVES 4–6

2 tbsp plain flour

1 chicken, weighing 1.6 kg/3 lb 8 oz,
    cut into 8 pieces

55 g/2 oz unsalted butter

1 tbsp sunflower oil

4 shallots, finely chopped

12 button mushrooms, sliced

2 tbsp brandy

500 ml/18 fl oz Riesling wine

250 ml/9 fl oz double cream

salt and pepper

cooked green vegetables,
    to serve

Method

1 Put the flour into a plastic food bag and season to taste. Add the chicken pieces, in batches, hold the top securely and shake well to coat. Transfer the chicken to a plate.

2 Heat half the butter with the oil in a heavy-based frying pan. Add the chicken pieces and cook over a medium–high heat, turning frequently, for 10 minutes, until golden all over. Using a slotted spoon, transfer them to a plate.

3 Wipe out the pan with kitchen paper, then return to a medium–high heat and melt the remaining butter. Add the shallots and mushrooms and cook, stirring constantly, for 3 minutes. Return the chicken to the frying pan and remove it from the heat. Warm the brandy in a small ladle, ignite and pour it over the chicken, shaking the pan gently until the flames have died down.

4 Return the pan to the heat and pour in the wine. Bring to the boil over a low heat, scraping up any sediment from the base of the pan. Transfer to the slow cooker, cover and cook on low for 5–6 hours, until the chicken is tender and cooked through.

5 Transfer the chicken to a serving dish and keep warm. Skim off any fat from the surface of the cooking liquid and pour the liquid into a saucepan. Stir in the cream and bring just to the boil over a low heat and pour over the chicken. Serve immediately with green vegetables.

33

Chicken Bonne Femme

SERVES 6

1 chicken, weighing 1.8 kg/4 lb

55 g/2 oz butter

2 tbsp olive oil

650 g/1 lb 7 oz small white onions,
    peeled

650 g/1 lb 7 oz small new potatoes

175 g/6 oz bacon, diced

500 ml/18 fl oz dry white wine

1 bouquet garni

500 ml/18 fl oz hot chicken stock

salt and pepper

chopped fresh flat-leaf parsley,
    to garnish

Method

1 Season the chicken inside and out with salt and pepper. Melt half the butter with the oil in a large frying pan. Add the chicken and cook over a medium heat, turning frequently, for 8–10 minutes, until evenly browned. Remove from the pan and put it into the slow cooker, breast-side down.

2 Add the onions, potatoes and bacon to the pan and cook, stirring frequently, for 10 minutes, until lightly browned. Pour in the wine, season to taste with salt and pepper and add the bouquet garni. Bring to the boil, then transfer the mixture to the slow cooker. Pour in the hot stock. Cover and cook, turning the chicken once halfway through cooking, for 5–6 hours, until the chicken is tender and cooked through.

3 Using a slotted spoon, transfer the vegetables and bacon to a warmed bowl. Carefully remove the chicken and put it on a warmed serving dish. Remove and discard the bouquet garni.

4 Measure 600 ml/1 pint of the cooking liquid, pour it into a saucepan and bring to the boil. Boil until slightly reduced, then whisk in the remaining butter, a little at a time. Pour the sauce into a sauceboat. Carve the chicken and transfer to individual plates with the bacon and vegetables. Garnish with parsley and serve immediately with the sauce.

34

Bulgarian Chicken

SERVES 6

2 tbsp sunflower oil

6 chicken portions

2 onions, chopped

2 garlic cloves, finely chopped

1 fresh red chilli, deseeded and finely
  chopped

6 tomatoes, peeled and chopped

2 tsp sweet paprika

1 bay leaf

225 ml/8 fl oz hot chicken stock

salt and pepper

Method

1 Heat the oil in a large heavy-based frying pan. Add the chicken and cook over a medium heat, turning occasionally, for about 10 minutes, until evenly browned.

2 Transfer the chicken to the slow cooker and add the onions, garlic, chilli and tomatoes. Sprinkle in the paprika, add the bay leaf and pour in the stock. Season to taste with salt and pepper. Stir well, cover and cook on low for 6 hours, until the chicken is cooked through and tender. Remove and discard the bay leaf. Transfer to warmed serving plates and serve immediately.

35

Chicken Parmigiana

SERVES 4

4 chicken portions, about 250 g/9 oz each

100 ml/3½ fl oz olive oil

3 red onions, thinly sliced

2 garlic cloves, finely chopped

1 red pepper, deseeded and thinly sliced

115 g/4 oz mushrooms, sliced

2 tsp chopped fresh thyme

1 tbsp chopped fresh flat-leaf parsley

400 g/14 oz canned chopped tomatoes

4 tbsp dry white vermouth

425 ml/15 fl oz chicken stock

85 g/3 oz Parmesan cheese, grated

salt and pepper

cooked pappardelle, to serve

Method

1 Season the chicken with salt and pepper to taste. Heat the oil in a large heavy-based saucepan. Add the chicken and cook over a medium heat for 5–6 minutes on each side, until evenly browned. Using tongs, transfer the chicken to the slow cooker.

2 Add the onions, garlic, red pepper, mushrooms, thyme, parsley, tomatoes, vermouth and stock to the pan. Season to taste with salt and pepper and bring to the boil, stirring occasionally. Transfer the mixture to the slow cooker, cover and cook on low for 8–9 hours, until the chicken is cooked through and tender.

3 Taste and adjust the seasoning, adding salt and pepper if needed. Transfer to warmed plates and sprinkle over the Parmesan. Serve immediately with pappardelle.

36

Nutty Chicken

SERVES 4

3 tbsp sunflower oil

4 skinless chicken portions

2 shallots, chopped

1 tsp ground ginger

1 tbsp plain flour

425 ml/15 fl oz beef stock

55 g/2 oz walnut pieces

grated rind of 1 lemon

2 tbsp lemon juice

1 tbsp black treacle

salt and pepper

pea shoots, to garnish

Method

1 Heat the oil in a large heavy-based frying pan. Season the chicken portions with salt and pepper to taste and add to the pan. Cook over a medium heat, turning occasionally, for 5–8 minutes, until lightly golden all over. Transfer to the slow cooker.

2 Add the shallots to the pan and cook, stirring occasionally, for 3–4 minutes, until softened. Sprinkle in the ginger and flour and cook, stirring constantly, for 1 minute. Gradually stir in the stock and bring to the boil, stirring constantly. Reduce the heat and simmer for 1 minute, then stir in the walnuts, lemon rind and juice and treacle.

3 Pour the sauce over the chicken. Cover and cook on low for 6 hours, until the chicken is cooked through and tender. Taste and adjust the seasoning, adding salt and pepper if needed. Transfer the chicken to warmed plates and spoon some of the sauce over each portion. Garnish with pea shoots and serve immediately.

37

Chicken Cacciatore

SERVES 4

3 tbsp olive oil

4 skinless chicken portions

2 onions, sliced

2 garlic cloves, finely chopped

400 g/14 oz canned chopped
   tomatoes

1 tbsp tomato purée

2 tbsp chopped fresh parsley

2 tsp fresh thyme leaves, plus extra
   sprigs to garnish

150 ml/5 fl oz red wine

salt and pepper

Method

1 Heat the oil in a heavy-based frying pan. Add the chicken and cook over a medium heat, turning occasionally, for 10 minutes, until golden all over. Using a slotted spoon, transfer the chicken to the slow cooker.

2 Add the onions to the pan and cook, stirring occasionally, for 5 minutes, until softened and just turning golden. Add the garlic, tomatoes, tomato purée, parsley, thyme leaves and wine. Season to taste with salt and pepper and bring to the boil.

3 Pour the tomato mixture over the chicken pieces. Cover and cook on low for 5 hours, until the chicken is tender and cooked through. Taste and adjust the seasoning, adding salt and pepper if needed. Transfer to warmed serving plates, garnish with thyme sprigs and serve immediately.

38

Chipotle Chicken

SERVES 4

4–6 dried chipotle chillies

4 garlic cloves, unpeeled

1 small onion, chopped

400 g/14 oz canned chopped
   tomatoes

300 ml/10 fl oz hot chicken or
   vegetable stock

4 skinless chicken breasts

salt and pepper

chopped fresh coriander,
   to garnish

Method

1 Preheat the oven to 200°C/400°F/Gas Mark 6. Place the chillies in a bowl and pour in just enough hot water to cover. Set aside to soak for 30 minutes. Meanwhile, place the unpeeled garlic cloves on a baking sheet and roast in the preheated oven for about 10 minutes, until soft. Remove from the oven and set aside to cool.

2 Drain the chillies, reserving 125 ml/4 fl oz of the soaking water. Deseed the chillies, if you like, and chop roughly. Place the chillies and reserved soaking water in a blender or food processor and process to a purée. Peel and mash the garlic in a bowl.

3 Place the chilli purée, garlic, onion and tomatoes in the slow cooker and stir in the stock. Season the chicken with salt and pepper to taste and place in the slow cooker. Cover and cook on low for about 5 hours, until the chicken is tender and cooked through.

4 Lift the chicken out of the slow cooker with a slotted spoon, cover and keep warm. Pour the cooking liquid into a saucepan and bring to the boil on the hob. Boil for 5–10 minutes, until reduced. Transfer the chicken to warmed serving plates and pour the sauce over the chicken. Serve immediately garnished with coriander.

39

Slow Roast Chicken

SERVES 4–6

1.5 kg/3 lb 5 oz oven-ready chicken
1/2 lemon
1 tbsp olive oil
1/2 tsp dried thyme
1/2 tsp paprika
salt and pepper

Method

1 Wipe the chicken with absorbent kitchen paper and tuck the lemon half inside the body cavity. Brush the oil over the chicken skin and sprinkle with thyme, paprika and salt and pepper, rubbing in with your fingers to cover all the skin.

2 Place the chicken in the slow cooker, cover and cook on high for 3 hours. Reduce the heat to low and cook for a further 4 hours, until the chicken is tender.

3 Carefully remove the chicken and place on a warmed platter, then skim any fat from the juices. Adjust the seasoning to taste and serve.

40

Chicken Quesadillas

SERVES 4

4 skinless chicken breast fillets

½ tsp crushed dried chillies

2 cloves garlic, crushed

2 tbsp finely chopped parsley

2 tbsp olive oil

350 g/12 oz cherry tomatoes

4 large wheat tortillas

250 g/9 oz mozzarella cheese

salt and pepper

Method

1 Place the chicken in a bowl with the chillies, garlic, parsley and 1 tbsp olive oil, and turn to coat evenly. Cover and leave in the refrigerator to marinate for at least 1 hour, or overnight.

2 Tip the tomatoes into the slow cooker and arrange the chicken breasts on top. Season with salt and pepper. Cover and cook on high for 2 hours, until tender.

3 Remove the chicken and shred the meat using two forks. Place on one side of each tortilla and top with the tomatoes. Chop or tear the mozzarella and arrange on top. Moisten the edges of the tortillas and fold over to enclose the filling.

4 Brush a griddle or large frying pan with the remaining oil and place over a medium heat. Add the quesadillas to the pan and cook until golden, turning once. Cut into wedges and serve. Any spare juices can be spooned over.

41

Barbecue Chicken

SERVES 4

8 skinless chicken drumsticks
or thighs

3 tbsp tomato purée

2 tbsp clear honey

1 tbsp Worcestershire sauce

juice of 1/2 lemon

1/2 tsp crushed dried chillies

1 garlic clove, crushed

salt and pepper

Method

1 Using a sharp knife, cut slashes into the thickest parts of the chicken flesh.

2 Mix the tomato purée, honey, Worcestershire sauce, lemon juice, chillies and garlic together and season with salt and pepper. Add the chicken and toss well to coat evenly.

3 Arrange the chicken in the slow cooker, cover and cook on high for 3 hours.

4 Remove the chicken with a slotted spoon and transfer to a warmed serving dish. Spoon the juices over the chicken, skimming off any fat. Serve immediately.

42

Sweet & Sour Chicken Wings

SERVES 4–6

1 kg/2 lb 4 oz chicken wings,
   tips removed

2 celery sticks, chopped

700 ml/1¼ pints hot chicken stock

2 tbsp cornflour

3 tbsp white wine vinegar or
   rice vinegar

3 tbsp dark soy sauce

5 tbsp sweet chilli sauce

55 g/2 oz soft light brown sugar

400 g/14 oz canned pineapple
   chunks in juice, drained

200 g/7 oz canned sliced bamboo
   shoots, drained and rinsed

½ green pepper, deseeded and
   thinly sliced

½ red pepper, deseeded and
   thinly sliced

salt

steamed pak choi, to serve

Method

1 Put the chicken wings and celery in the slow cooker and season well with salt. Pour in the stock, cover and cook on low for 5 hours.

2 Drain the chicken wings, reserving 350 ml/12 fl oz of the stock, and keep warm. Pour the reserved stock into a saucepan and stir in the cornflour. Add the vinegar, soy sauce and chilli sauce. Place over a medium heat and stir in the sugar. Cook, stirring constantly, for 5 minutes, or until the sugar has dissolved completely and the sauce is thickened, smooth and clear.

3 Reduce the heat, stir in the pineapple, bamboo shoots and peppers and simmer gently for 2–3 minutes. Stir in the chicken wings until they are thoroughly coated, then transfer to warmed serving bowls. Serve immediately with pak choi.

43

Easy Chinese Chicken

SERVES 4

2 tsp grated fresh ginger

4 garlic cloves, finely chopped

2 star anise

150 ml/5 fl oz Chinese rice wine or medium-dry sherry

2 tbsp dark soy sauce

1 tsp sesame oil

5 tbsp water

4 skinless chicken thighs or drumsticks

shredded spring onions, to garnish

cooked rice, to serve

Method

1 Mix together the ginger, garlic, star anise, rice wine, soy sauce, sesame oil and water in a bowl. Place the chicken in a saucepan, add the spice mixture and bring to the boil.

2 Transfer to the slow cooker, cover and cook on low for 4 hours, or until the chicken is tender and cooked through.

3 Remove and discard the star anise. Transfer the chicken to warmed serving plates, garnish with shredded spring onions and serve immediately with rice.

44

Parmesan Chicken

SERVES 4

1 egg, beaten

4 skinless, boneless chicken breasts

85 g/3 oz fine dry breadcrumbs

2 tbsp olive oil

350 g/12 oz ready-prepared
   tomato-based pasta sauce

4 thin slices Cheddar cheese

115 g/4 oz finely grated Parmesan
   cheese

salt and pepper

cooked rice, to serve

Method

1 Season the egg with salt and pepper. Dip each chicken breast in the egg, turning to coat evenly, then dip into the breadcrumbs, lightly pressing down to cover evenly.

2 Heat the oil in a frying pan over a high heat, add the chicken breasts and fry quickly for 3–4 minutes, until golden brown, turning once.

3 Pour the pasta sauce into the slow cooker and place the chicken breasts on top. Cover and cook on low for 4 hours.

4 Place a slice of Cheddar cheese on top of each chicken breast and sprinkle with Parmesan cheese. Cover and cook on high for a further 20 minutes. Transfer to a warmed serving dish and serve immediately with rice.

45

Chicken Braised with Cabbage

SERVES 4

2 tbsp sunflower oil

4 skinless chicken thighs
   or drumsticks

1 onion, chopped

500 g/1 lb 2 oz red cabbage,
   cored and shredded

2 apples, peeled and chopped

12 canned or cooked chestnuts,
   halved (optional)

1/2 tsp juniper berries

125 ml/4 fl oz red wine

salt and pepper

chopped fresh flat-leaf parsley,
   to garnish

Method

1 Heat the oil in a large heavy-based saucepan. Add the chicken and cook, turning frequently, for 5 minutes, until golden on all sides. Using a slotted spoon, transfer to a plate lined with kitchen paper.

2 Add the onion to the saucepan and cook over a medium heat, stirring occasionally, until softened. Stir in the cabbage and apples and cook, stirring occasionally, for 5 minutes. Add the chestnuts, if using, juniper berries and wine and season to taste with salt and pepper. Bring to the boil.

3 Spoon half the cabbage mixture into the slow cooker, add the chicken pieces, then top with the remaining cabbage mixture. Cover and cook on low for 5 hours, until the chicken is tender and cooked through. Transfer to warmed serving bowls, garnish with parsley and serve immediately.

46

Turkey Meatloaf

SERVES 4

oil for greasing

600 g/1 lb 5 oz turkey mince

1 onion, finely chopped

55 g/2 oz porridge oats

2 tbsp chopped fresh sage

2 tbsp Worcestershire sauce

1 egg, beaten

salt and pepper

Method

1 Grease and line a 900-g/2-lb loaf tin, or a tin that fits into your slow cooker.

2 Mix together the turkey mince, onion, oats, sage, Worcestershire sauce, egg, salt and pepper.

3 Spoon the mixture into the tin and smooth the top level with a palette knife.

4 Place the loaf in the slow cooker and place a piece of baking paper on top. Cover and cook on low for 4 hours, until firm and the juices are clear, not pink.

5 Turn out the loaf and serve sliced.

47

Turkey & Rice Casserole

SERVES 4

1 tbsp olive oil

500 g/1 lb 2 oz diced
   turkey breast

1 onion, diced

2 carrots, diced

2 celery sticks, sliced

250 g/9 oz closed-cup mushrooms,
   sliced

175 g/6 oz long-grain rice,
   preferably Basmati

450 ml/16 fl oz hot chicken stock

salt and pepper

Method

1 Heat the oil in a heavy-based frying pan, add the turkey and fry over a high heat for 3–4 minutes, until lightly browned.

2 Combine the onion, carrots, celery, mushrooms and rice in the slow cooker. Arrange the turkey on top, season well with salt and pepper and pour the stock over. Cover and cook on high for 2 hours.

3 Stir lightly with a fork to mix, adjust the seasoning to taste and serve immediately.

48

Turkey Hash

SERVES 4

1 tbsp olive oil

500 g/1 lb 2 oz turkey mince

1 large red onion, diced

550 g/1 lb 4 oz butternut squash, diced

2 celery sticks, sliced

500 g/1 lb 2 oz potatoes, peeled and diced

3 tbsp Worcestershire sauce

2 bay leaves

salt and pepper

Method

1 Heat the oil in a frying pan, add the turkey and fry over a high heat, stirring, until broken up and lightly browned.

2 Place all the vegetables in the slow cooker then add the turkey and pan juices. Add the Worcestershire sauce and bay leaves and season with salt and pepper. Cover and cook on low for 7 hours. Transfer to warmed serving bowls and serve immediately.

49

Pesto Turkey Pasta

SERVES 4

250 g/9 oz dried macaroni

175 ml/6 fl oz tomato juice

500 g/1 lb 2 oz turkey mince

1 small onion, finely chopped

40 g/1½ oz fresh white breadcrumbs

100 g/3½ oz pesto sauce

125 g/4½ oz mozzarella cheese

salt and pepper

fresh basil leaves, to garnish

Method

1 Bring a large saucepan of lightly salted water to the boil, add the pasta, return to the boil and cook for half the amount of time stated on the pack (5–6 minutes). Drain well, place in the slow cooker and stir in the tomato juice.

2 Mix the turkey, onion and breadcrumbs together. Season well with salt and pepper. Divide the mixture into about 20 small balls, rolling them with your hands.

3 Arrange the meatballs over the pasta in a single layer and spoon a little of the pesto sauce on top of each. Cover and cook on high for 2 hours.

4 Tear the mozzarella cheese into small pieces and scatter over the meatballs. Cover and cook on high for a further 20 minutes. Serve immediately, garnished with fresh basil.

3

FISH & SEAFOOD

50

New England Clam Chowder

SERVES 4

25 g/1 oz butter

1 onion, finely chopped

2 potatoes, peeled and
    cut into cubes

1 large carrot, diced

400 ml/14 fl oz fish stock or water

280 g/10 oz canned clams, drained

250 ml/9 fl oz double cream

salt and pepper

chopped fresh parsley, to garnish

fresh crusty bread, to serve

Method

1 Melt the butter in a frying pan, add the onion and fry over a medium heat for 4–5 minutes, stirring, until golden.

2 Transfer the onion to the slow cooker with the potatoes, carrot, stock and salt and pepper. Cover and cook on high for 3 hours.

3 Add the clams and the cream to the slow cooker and stir to mix evenly. Cover and cook for a further 1 hour.

4 Adjust the seasoning to taste. Transfer to warmed serving bowls, sprinkle with parsley and serve immediately with crusty bread.

51

Salmon Chowder

SERVES 4

15 g/½ oz butter

1 tbsp sunflower oil

1 onion, finely chopped

1 leek, finely chopped

1 fennel bulb, finely chopped,
  feathery tops reserved

280 g/10 oz potatoes, diced

700 ml/1¼ pints fish stock

450 g/1 lb salmon fillet, skinned and
  cut into cubes

300 ml/10 fl oz milk

150 ml/5 fl oz single cream

2 tbsp chopped fresh dill

salt and pepper

Method

1 Melt the butter with the oil in a saucepan. Add the onion, leek and fennel and cook over a low heat, stirring occasionally, for 5 minutes. Add the potatoes and cook, stirring occasionally, for a further 4 minutes, then pour in the stock and season to taste with salt and pepper. Bring to the boil, then transfer to the slow cooker. Cover and cook on low for 3 hours, until the potatoes are tender.

2 Meanwhile, chop the fennel fronds and set aside. Add the salmon to the slow cooker, pour in the milk and stir gently. Re-cover and cook on low for 30 minutes, until the fish flakes easily.

3 Gently stir in the cream, dill and the reserved fennel fronds, re-cover and cook for a further 10–15 minutes, until heated through. Taste and adjust the seasoning, adding salt and pepper if needed. Serve immediately.

52

Salmon with Dill & Lime

SERVES 4

40 g/1½ oz butter, melted

1 onion, thinly sliced

450 g/1 lb potatoes, peeled and thinly sliced

100 ml/3½ fl oz hot fish stock or water

4 pieces skinless salmon fillet, about 140 g/5 oz each

juice of 1 lime

2 tbsp chopped fresh dill

salt and pepper

lime wedges, to serve

Method

1 Brush the base of the slow cooker with 1 tablespoon of the butter. Layer the onion and potatoes in the dish, sprinkling with salt and pepper between the layers. Add the stock and drizzle with 1 tablespoon of the butter. Cover and cook on low for 3 hours.

2 Arrange the salmon over the vegetables in a single layer. Drizzle the lime juice over, sprinkle with dill and salt and pepper and pour the remaining butter on top. Cover and cook on low for a further 1 hour, until the fish flakes easily.

3 Serve the salmon and vegetables on warmed plates with the juices spooned over and lime wedges on the side.

53

Salmon Florentine

SERVES 4

150 ml/5 fl oz fish stock

225 ml/8 fl oz dry white wine

2 lemons

1 onion, thinly sliced

4 salmon fillets, about
175 g/6 oz each

1 bouquet garni

1.3 kg/3 lb spinach, coarse stalks
removed

freshly grated nutmeg, to taste

175 g/6 oz unsalted butter,
plus extra for greasing

salt and pepper

Method

1 Lightly grease the slow cooker pot with butter. Pour the stock and wine into a saucepan and bring to the boil. Meanwhile, thinly slice one of the lemons. Put half the lemon slices and all the onion slices over the base of the slow cooker pot and top with the salmon fillets. Season to taste with salt and pepper, add the bouquet garni and cover the fish with the remaining lemon slices. Pour the hot stock mixture over the fish, cover and cook on low for 1$^{1}/_{2}$ hours, until the fish flakes easily.

2 Meanwhile, finely grate the rind and squeeze the juice from the remaining lemon. When the fish is nearly ready, cook the spinach, in just the water clinging to the leaves after washing, for 3–5 minutes, until wilted. Drain well, squeezing out as much water as possible. Chop finely, arrange on a warmed serving dish and season to taste with salt, pepper and nutmeg.

3 Carefully lift the fish out of the slow cooker with a fish slice and discard the lemon slices, onion slices and bouquet garni. Put the salmon fillets on the bed of spinach and keep warm.

4 Melt the butter in a saucepan over a low heat. Stir in the lemon rind and half the juice. Taste and adjust the seasoning, adding more lemon juice, salt and pepper if needed. Pour the lemon butter sauce over the fish and serve immediately.

54

Sea Bream in Lemon Sauce

SERVES 4

8 sea bream fillets

55 g/2 oz unsalted butter

25 g/1 oz plain flour

850 ml/1½ pints warm milk

4 tbsp lemon juice

225 g/8 oz mushrooms, sliced

1 bouquet garni

salt and pepper

lemon wedges and griddled
  asparagus, to serve

Method

1 Put the fish fillets into the slow cooker and set aside.

2 Melt the butter in a saucepan over a low heat. Add the flour and cook, stirring constantly, for 1 minute. Gradually stir in the milk, a little at a time, and bring to the boil, stirring constantly. Stir in the lemon juice and mushrooms, add the bouquet garni and season to taste with salt and pepper. Reduce the heat and simmer for 5 minutes. Pour the sauce over the fish fillets, cover and cook on low for 1½ hours.

3 Carefully lift out the fish fillets and transfer to warmed serving plates. Serve immediately with lemon wedges and asparagus.

55

Moroccan Sea Bass

SERVES 2

2 tbsp olive oil

2 onions, chopped

2 garlic cloves, finely chopped

2 carrots, finely chopped

1 fennel bulb, finely chopped

1/2 tsp ground cumin

1/2 tsp ground cloves

1 tsp ground coriander

pinch of saffron threads

300 ml/10 fl oz fish stock

1 preserved or fresh lemon

900 g/2 lb sea bass, cleaned

salt and pepper

Method

1 Heat the oil in a large heavy-based saucepan. Add the onions, garlic, carrots and fennel and cook over a medium heat, stirring occasionally, for 5 minutes. Stir in all the spices and cook, stirring, for a further 2 minutes. Pour in the stock, season to taste with salt and pepper and bring to the boil.

2 Transfer the mixture to the slow cooker. Cover and cook on low for 6 hours, or until the vegetables are tender.

3 Rinse the preserved lemon. Discard the fish head, if you like. Slice the lemon and place the slices in the fish cavity, then place the fish in the slow cooker on top of the vegetables. Re-cover and cook on high for 30–45 minutes, until the flesh flakes easily.

4 Carefully transfer the fish to a platter and spoon the vegetables around it, using a slotted spoon. Cover and keep warm. Transfer the cooking liquid to a saucepan and boil for a few minutes, until reduced. Spoon it over the fish and serve immediately.

56

Red Snapper with Fennel

SERVES 4

4 red snapper, about
    350 g/12 oz each, cleaned

1 orange, halved and thinly sliced

2 garlic cloves, thinly sliced

6 fresh thyme sprigs

1 tbsp olive oil

1 fennel bulb, thinly sliced

450 ml/16 fl oz orange juice

1 bay leaf

1 tsp dill seeds

salt and pepper

salad leaves, to serve

Method

1 Season the fish inside and outside with salt and pepper.
Make 3–4 diagonal slashes on each side. Divide the orange
slices between the cavities and add 2–3 garlic slices and a
thyme sprig to each. Put the remaining garlic and thyme in
the slashes.

2 Heat the oil in a large frying pan. Add the fennel and
cook over a medium heat, stirring frequently, for 3–5 minutes,
until just softened. Add the orange juice and bay leaf and
bring to the boil, then reduce the heat and simmer for a
further 5 minutes.

3 Transfer the fennel mixture to the slow cooker. Put the fish
on top and sprinkle with the dill seeds. Cover and cook on high
for 1 1/4–1 1/2 hours, until the flesh flakes easily.

4 Carefully transfer the fish to warmed individual plates.
Remove and discard the bay leaf. Spoon the fennel and some
of the cooking juices over the fish and serve immediately with
salad leaves.

57

Pollock Bake

SERVES 4

1 tbsp olive oil

1 red onion, sliced

1 yellow pepper, deseeded and sliced

4 pollock fillets
   (about 140 g/5 oz each)

2 tomatoes, thinly sliced

8 stoned black olives, halved

1 garlic clove, thinly sliced

2 tsp balsamic vinegar

juice of 1 orange

salt and pepper

Method

1 Heat the oil in a frying pan, add the onion and yellow pepper and fry over a high heat for 3–4 minutes, stirring, until lightly browned. Transfer to the slow cooker, cover and cook on high for 1 hour.

2 Arrange the fish fillets over the vegetables and season with salt and pepper. Arrange a layer of tomatoes and olives over the top and sprinkle with the garlic, vinegar and salt and pepper. Pour over the orange juice, cover and cook on high for a further 1 hour. Transfer to warmed serving plates and serve immediately.

58

Sole & Prawn Cream

SERVES 4

900 g/2 lb potatoes, cut into chunks

700 g/1 lb 9 oz sole fillets

25 g/1 oz butter, plus extra
for greasing

2 egg yolks

175 g/6 oz Cheddar cheese, grated

1 tbsp chopped fresh flat-leaf
parsley, plus extra sprigs
to garnish

550 g/1 lb 4 oz cooked peeled
prawns

salt and pepper

Method

1 Put the potatoes into a saucepan, pour in water to cover, add a pinch of salt and bring to the boil. Reduce the heat, cover and cook for 20–25 minutes, until soft but not falling apart.

2 Meanwhile, grease a 1.2-litre/2-pint pudding basin with butter, then line it with the fish fillets, skin-side inwards and with the tail ends overlapping the rim. Cut out a double round of greaseproof paper that is 5 cm/2 inches wider than the rim of the basin. Grease one side with butter.

3 Drain the potatoes in a colander. Return to the saucepan, add the butter and reheat gently until it has melted. Remove from the heat and mash well, then stir in the egg yolks, cheese and chopped parsley. Season lightly with salt and pepper.

4 Make alternating layers of the mashed potato mixture and prawns in the pudding basin, then fold over the overlapping fish fillets. Cover the basin with the greaseproof paper rounds and tie in place with string.

5 Stand the basin on a trivet in the slow cooker and pour in enough boiling water to come about halfway up the side. Cover and cook on low for 2 1/2 hours.

6 Carefully remove the basin from the slow cooker and discard the greaseproof paper. Turn out onto a warmed serving dish. Garnish with parsley sprigs and serve immediately.

59

Tagliatelle with Tuna

SERVES 4

200 g/7 oz dried egg tagliatelle

400 g/14 oz canned tuna steak
  in oil, drained

1 bunch spring onions, sliced

175 g/6 oz frozen peas

2 tsp hot chilli sauce

600 ml/1 pint hot chicken stock

115 g/4 oz grated Cheddar cheese

salt and pepper

Method

1 Bring a large saucepan of lightly salted water to the boil. Add the pasta, return to the boil and cook for 2 minutes, until the pasta ribbons are loose. Drain.

2 Break up the tuna into bite-sized chunks and place in the slow cooker with the pasta, spring onions and peas. Season to taste with salt and pepper.

3 Add the chilli sauce to the stock and pour over the ingredients in the slow cooker. Sprinkle the grated cheese over the top. Cover and cook on low for 2 hours. Serve immediately on warmed plates.

60

French-Style Fish Stew

SERVES 4–6

large pinch of saffron threads

1 prepared squid

900 g/2 lb mixed white fish, such as sea bass or monkfish, filleted and cut into large chunks

24 large raw prawns, peeled and deveined, heads and shells reserved

2 tbsp olive oil

1 large onion, finely chopped

1 fennel bulb, thinly sliced, feathery fronds reserved

2 large garlic cloves, crushed

4 tbsp Pernod

1 litre/1¾ pints fish stock

400 g/14 oz canned chopped tomatoes, drained

1 tbsp tomato purée

1 bay leaf

pinch of sugar

salt and pepper

Method

1 Toast the saffron threads in a dry frying pan over a high heat, for 1 minute. Set side. Cut off and reserve the tentacles from the squid and slice the body into 5-mm/¼-inch rings. Place the seafood and fish in a bowl, cover and chill in the refrigerator until required. Tie the heads and shells of the prawns in a piece of muslin.

2 Heat the oil in a frying pan. Add the onion and fennel and cook over a low heat, for 5 minutes. Add the garlic and cook for 2 minutes. Remove the pan from the heat. Heat the Pernod in a saucepan, ignite and pour it over the onion and fennel, gently shaking the frying pan until the flames have died down.

3 Return the frying pan to the heat, stir in the toasted saffron, stock, tomatoes, tomato purée, bay leaf and sugar, and season with salt and pepper. Bring to the boil, then transfer to the slow cooker, add the bag of prawn shells, cover and cook on low for 6 hours.

4 Remove and discard the bag of prawn shells and the bay leaf. Add the fish and seafood to the slow cooker, cover and cook on high for 30 minutes until the fish flakes easily. Serve garnished with the reserved fennel fronds.

61

Shellfish Stew

SERVES 8

1 tbsp olive oil

115 g/4 oz bacon, diced

2 tbsp butter

2 shallots, chopped

2 leeks, sliced

2 celery sticks, chopped

2 potatoes, diced

675 g/1 lb 8 oz tomatoes, peeled,
    deseeded and chopped

3 tbsp chopped fresh parsley

3 tbsp snipped fresh chives,
    plus extra to garnish

1 bay leaf

1 fresh thyme sprig

1.4 litres/2½ pints fish stock

24 live mussels

24 live clams

450 g/1 lb sea bream fillets

24 raw tiger prawns

salt and pepper

Method

1 Heat the oil in a heavy-based frying pan. Add the bacon and cook, stirring frequently, for 5–8 minutes until crisp. Using a slotted spoon, transfer to the slow cooker. Add the butter to the frying pan and when it has melted, add the shallots, leeks, celery and potatoes. Cook over a low heat, stirring occasionally, for 5 minutes until softened. Stir in the tomatoes, parsley, chives, bay leaf and thyme, pour in the stock and bring to the boil, stirring constantly. Pour the mixture into the slow cooker, cover and cook on low for 7 hours.

2 Meanwhile, scrub the mussels and clams under cold running water and pull off the 'beards' from the mussels. Discard any with broken shells or that do not shut immediately when sharply tapped. Cut the fish fillets into bite-sized chunks. Peel and devein the prawns.

3 Remove the bay leaf and thyme sprig from the stew and discard. Season with salt and pepper and add all the fish and seafood. Re-cover and cook on high for 30 minutes. Discard any shellfish that remain closed. Serve garnished with extra chives.

62

Louisiana Gumbo

SERVES 6

2 tbsp sunflower oil

175 g/6 oz okra, trimmed and
cut into 2.5-cm/1-inch pieces

2 onions, finely chopped

4 celery sticks, very finely chopped

1 garlic clove, finely chopped

2 tbsp plain flour

1/2 tsp sugar

1 tsp ground cumin

700ml/1 1/4 pints fish stock

1 red pepper, deseeded and chopped

1 green pepper, deseeded and
chopped

2 large tomatoes, chopped

4 tbsp chopped fresh parsley

1 tbsp chopped fresh coriander

Tabasco sauce

350 g/12 oz large raw prawns,
peeled and deveined

350 g/12 oz cod or haddock fillets,
skinned and cut into 2.5-cm/
1-inch chunks

350 g/12 oz monkfish fillet,
cut into 2.5-cm/1-inch chunks

salt and pepper

Method

1 Heat half the oil in a heavy-based frying pan. Add the okra and cook over a low heat, stirring frequently, for 5 minutes until browned. Using a slotted spoon, transfer the okra to the slow cooker.

2 Add the remaining oil to the frying pan. Add the onions and celery and cook over a low heat, stirring occasionally, for 5 minutes until softened. Add the garlic and cook, stirring frequently, for 1 minute, then sprinkle in the flour, sugar and cumin and season with salt and pepper. Cook, stirring constantly, for 2 minutes, then remove the frying pan from the heat.

3 Gradually stir in the stock, then return the pan to the heat and bring to the boil, stirring constantly. Pour the mixture over the okra and stir in the peppers and tomatoes. Cover and cook on low for 5–6 hours.

4 Stir in the parsley, coriander and Tabasco to taste, then add the prawns, cod and monkfish. Cover and cook on high for 30 minutes until the fish is cooked and the prawns have changed colour. Taste and adjust the seasoning if necessary and serve.

63

Jambalaya

SERVES 4

1/2 tsp cayenne pepper

2 tsp chopped fresh thyme

350 g/12 oz skinless, boneless
chicken breasts, diced

2 tbsp corn oil

2 onions, chopped

2 garlic cloves, finely chopped

2 green peppers, deseeded and
chopped

2 celery sticks, chopped

115 g/4 oz smoked ham, chopped

175 g/6 oz chorizo sausage, sliced

400 g/14 oz canned chopped
tomatoes

2 tbsp tomato purée

225 ml/8 fl oz chicken stock

450 g/1 lb raw prawns, peeled and
deveined

450 g/1 lb cooked rice

salt and pepper

snipped fresh chives, to garnish

Method

1 Mix together the cayenne pepper, 1/2 teaspoon of pepper,
1 teaspoon of salt and the thyme in a bowl. Add the chicken
and toss to coat.

2 Heat the oil in a large heavy-based saucepan. Add the
onions, garlic, green peppers and celery and cook over a low
heat, stirring occasionally, for 5 minutes. Add the chicken and
cook over a medium heat, stirring frequently, for a further
5 minutes, until golden all over. Stir in the ham, chorizo,
tomatoes, tomato purée and stock and bring to the boil.

3 Transfer the mixture to the slow cooker. Cover and cook on
low for 6 hours. Add the prawns and rice, re-cover and cook on
high for 30 minutes.

4 Taste and adjust the seasoning, adding salt and pepper if
necessary. Transfer to warmed plates, garnish with chives and
serve immediately.

64

Bouillabaisse

SERVES 6

2.25 kg/5 lb mixed white fish,
  such as red mullet, sea bream,
  sea bass, monkfish and whiting,
  filleted and bones and heads
  reserved, if possible

450 g/1 lb raw prawns

grated rind of 1 orange

pinch of saffron threads

4 garlic cloves, finely chopped

225 ml/8 fl oz olive oil

2 onions, finely chopped

1 leek, thinly sliced

4 potatoes, thinly sliced

2 large tomatoes, peeled
  and chopped

1 bunch fresh flat-leaf parsley,
  chopped

1 fresh fennel sprig

1 fresh thyme sprig

1 bay leaf

2 cloves

6 black peppercorns

1 strip thinly pared
  orange rind

sea salt

lightly toasted crusty bread,
  to serve

Method

1 Cut the fish fillets into bite-sized pieces. Peel and devein the prawns, reserving the heads and shells. Rinse the fish bones, if using, and cut away the gills from the fish heads. Place the chunks of fish and the prawns in a large bowl. Sprinkle with the grated orange rind, saffron, half the garlic and 2 tablespoons of the oil. Cover and set aside in the refrigerator.

2 Put the remaining garlic, the onions, leek, potatoes, tomatoes, parsley, fennel, thyme, bay leaf, cloves, peppercorns and strip of orange rind into the slow cooker. Add the fish heads and bones, if using, and the prawn shells and heads. Pour in the remaining oil and enough boiling water to cover the ingredients by 2.5 cm/1 inch. Season to taste with sea salt. Cover and cook on low for 8 hours.

3 Strain the stock and return the liquid to the slow cooker. Discard the flavourings, fish and prawn trimmings but reserve the vegetables and return them to the slow cooker if you like. Add the fish and prawn mixture, re-cover and cook on high for 30 minutes, until the fish is cooked through and flakes easily.

4 Ladle into warmed bowls and serve immediately with toasted crusty bread.

65

South-Western Seafood Stew

SERVES 4

2 tbsp olive oil, plus extra
   for drizzling

1 large onion, chopped

4 garlic cloves, finely chopped

1 yellow pepper, deseeded and
   chopped

1 red pepper, deseeded and chopped

1 orange pepper, deseeded
   and chopped

450 g/1 lb tomatoes, peeled
   and chopped

2 large mild green chillies, such as
   poblano, chopped

finely grated rind and
   juice of 1 lime

2 tbsp chopped fresh coriander,
   plus extra leaves to garnish

1 bay leaf

450 ml/16 fl oz fish, vegetable or
   chicken stock

450 g/1 lb red mullet fillets

450 g/1 lb raw prawns

225 g/8 oz prepared squid

salt and pepper

Method

1 Heat the oil in a saucepan. Add the onion and garlic and cook over a low heat, stirring occasionally, for 5 minutes, until softened. Add the peppers, tomatoes and chillies and cook, stirring frequently, for 5 minutes. Stir in the lime rind and juice, add the chopped coriander and bay leaf and pour in the stock. Bring to the boil, stirring occasionally.

2 Transfer the mixture to the slow cooker, cover and cook on low for 7 1/2 hours. Meanwhile, skin the fish fillets, if necessary, and cut the flesh into chunks. Peel and devein the prawns. Cut the squid bodies into rings and halve the tentacles or leave them whole.

3 Add the seafood to the stew, season to taste with salt and pepper, re-cover and cook on high for 30 minutes, or until tender and cooked through. Remove and discard the bay leaf. Transfer to warmed serving bowls, garnish with coriander leaves and serve immediately.

66

Seafood in Saffron Sauce

SERVES 4

2 tbsp olive oil

1 onion, sliced

2 celery sticks, sliced

pinch of saffron threads

1 tbsp chopped fresh thyme

2 garlic cloves, finely chopped

800 g/1 lb 12 oz canned chopped
    tomatoes, drained

175 ml/6 fl oz dry white wine

2 litres/3½ pints fish stock

225 g/8 oz live clams

225 g/8 oz live mussels

350 g/12 oz red mullet fillets

450 g/1 lb monkfish fillet

225 g/8 oz squid rings, thawed
    if frozen

2 tbsp shredded fresh basil leaves

salt and pepper

Method

1 Heat the oil in a heavy-based frying pan. Add the onion, celery, saffron, thyme and a pinch of salt and cook over a low heat, stirring occasionally, for 5 minutes until softened. Add the garlic and cook, stirring constantly, for 2 minutes.

2 Add the tomatoes, wine and stock, season with salt and pepper and bring to the boil, stirring constantly. Transfer the mixture to the slow cooker, cover and cook on low for 5 hours.

3 Meanwhile, scrub the shellfish under cold running water and pull the 'beards' off the mussels. Discard any with broken shells or that do not shut immediately when sharply tapped. Cut the mullet and monkfish fillets into bite-sized chunks.

4 Add the pieces of fish, the shellfish and the squid rings to the slow cooker, re-cover and cook on high for 30 minutes until the clams and mussels have opened and the fish is cooked through. Discard any shellfish that remain closed. Stir in the basil and serve.

67

Tagliatelle with Prawns

SERVES 4

400 g/14 oz tomatoes, peeled and chopped

140 g/5 oz tomato purée

1 garlic clove, finely chopped

2 tbsp chopped fresh parsley

500 g/1 lb 2 oz cooked, peeled Mediterranean prawns

6 fresh basil leaves, torn, plus extra to garnish

400 g/14 oz dried tagliatelle

salt and pepper

Method

1 Put the tomatoes, tomato purée, garlic and parsley in the slow cooker and season with salt and pepper. Cover and cook on low for 7 hours.

2 Add the prawns and basil. Re-cover and cook on high for 15 minutes.

3 Meanwhile, bring a large saucepan of lightly salted water to the boil. Add the pasta, bring back to the boil and cook for 10–12 minutes until tender but still firm to the bite.

4 Drain the pasta and tip it into a warm serving bowl. Add the prawn sauce and toss lightly with 2 large forks. Garnish with the basil leaves and serve immediately.

4

VEGETARIAN

68

Tomato & Lentil Soup

SERVES 4

2 tbsp sunflower oil

1 onion, chopped

1 garlic clove, finely chopped

2 celery sticks, chopped

2 carrots, chopped

1 tsp ground cumin

1 tsp ground coriander

175 g/6 oz red or yellow lentils

1 tbsp tomato purée

1.2 litres/2 pints vegetable stock

400 g/14 oz canned chopped
   tomatoes

1 bay leaf

salt and pepper

crème fraîche and toasted crusty
   bread, to serve

Method

1 Heat the oil in a saucepan. Add the onion and garlic and cook over a low heat, stirring occasionally, for 5 minutes, until softened. Stir in the celery and carrots and cook, stirring occasionally, for a further 4 minutes. Stir in the ground cumin and coriander and cook, stirring, for 1 minute, then add the lentils.

2 Mix the tomato purée with a little of the stock in a small bowl and add to the pan with the remaining stock, the tomatoes and bay leaf. Bring to the boil, then transfer to the slow cooker. Stir well, cover and cook on low for $3^{1}/_{2}$ –4 hours.

3 Remove and discard the bay leaf. Transfer the soup to a food processor or blender and process until smooth. Season to taste with salt and pepper. Ladle into warmed soup bowls, top each with a swirl of crème fraîche and serve immediately with toasted crusty bread.

69

Carrot & Coriander Soup

SERVES 6

1 tbsp butter

1 1/2 tbsp sunflower oil

1 Spanish onion, finely chopped

500 g/1 lb 2 oz carrots, diced

1-cm/1/2-inch piece fresh ginger

2 tsp ground coriander

1 tsp plain flour

1.2 litres/2 pints vegetable stock

150 ml/5 fl oz soured cream

2 tbsp chopped fresh coriander

salt and pepper

croûtons, to serve

Method

1 Melt the butter with the oil in a saucepan. Add the onion, carrots and ginger, cover and cook over a low heat, stirring occasionally, for 8 minutes, until softened and just beginning to colour.

2 Sprinkle over the ground coriander and flour and cook, stirring constantly, for 1 minute. Gradually stir in the stock, a little at a time, and bring to the boil, stirring constantly. Season to taste with salt and pepper.

3 Transfer the mixture to the slow cooker, cover and cook on low for 4–5 hours. Ladle the soup into a food processor or blender, in batches if necessary, and process until smooth. Return the soup to the slow cooker and stir in the soured cream. Cover and cook on low for a further 15–20 minutes, until heated through.

4 Ladle the soup into warmed soup bowls, garnish with the chopped coriander and sprinkle with croûtons. Serve immediately.

70

Greek Bean & Vegetable Soup

SERVES 4–6

500g/1 lb 2 oz dried haricot beans,
   soaked in cold water overnight

2 onions, finely chopped

2 garlic cloves, finely chopped

2 potatoes, chopped

2 carrots, chopped

2 tomatoes, peeled and chopped

2 celery sticks, chopped

4 tbsp extra virgin olive oil

1 bay leaf

salt and pepper

12 black olives and 2 tbsp chopped
   fresh chives, to garnish

Method

1 Drain the beans and rinse well under cold running water. Place them in the slow cooker and add the onions, garlic, potatoes, carrots, tomatoes, celery, olive oil and bay leaf.

2 Pour in 2 litres/3½ pints boiling water, making sure that all the ingredients are fully submerged. Cover and cook on low for 12 hours until the beans are tender.

3 Remove and discard the bay leaf. Season the soup to taste with salt and pepper and garnish with the olives and chives. Transfer into warm soup bowls and serve.

71

Louisiana Courgettes

SERVES 6

1 kg/2 lb 4 oz courgettes,
  thickly sliced

1 onion, finely chopped

2 garlic cloves, finely chopped

2 red peppers, deseeded
  and chopped

5 tbsp hot vegetable stock

4 tomatoes, peeled and chopped

25 g/1 oz butter, diced

salt and cayenne pepper

crusty bread, to serve

Method

1 Place the courgettes, onion, garlic and red peppers in the slow cooker and season to taste with salt and cayenne pepper. Pour in the stock and mix well.

2 Sprinkle the chopped tomatoes on top and dot with the butter. Cover and cook on high for 2 1/2 hours until tender. Serve immediately with crusty bread.

72

Warm Chickpea Salad

SERVES 6

225 g/8 oz dried chickpeas, soaked overnight in cold water and drained

115 g/4 oz stoned black olives

4 spring onions, finely chopped

fresh parsley sprigs, to garnish

crusty bread, to serve

Dressing

2 tbsp red wine vinegar

2 tbsp mixed chopped fresh herbs, such as parsley, rosemary and thyme

3 garlic cloves, very finely chopped

125 ml/4 fl oz extra virgin olive oil

salt and pepper

Method

1 Place the chickpeas in the slow cooker and add sufficient boiling water to cover. Cover and cook on low for 12 hours.

2 Drain well and transfer to a bowl. Stir in the olives and spring onions.

3 To make the dressing, whisk together the vinegar, herbs and garlic in a jug and season with salt and pepper to taste. Gradually whisk in the olive oil. Pour the dressing over the still-warm chickpeas and toss lightly to coat. Garnish with the parsley sprigs and serve warm with crusty bread.

73

Winter Vegetable Medley

SERVES 4

2 tbsp sunflower oil

2 onions, peeled and chopped

3 carrots, chopped

3 parsnips, chopped

2 bunches celery, chopped

2 tbsp chopped fresh parsley

1 tbsp chopped fresh coriander

300 ml/10 fl oz vegetable stock

salt and pepper

Method

1 Heat the oil in a large, heavy-based saucepan. Add the onions and cook over a medium heat, stirring occasionally, for 5 minutes until softened. Add the carrots, parsnips and celery and cook, stirring occasionally, for a further 5 minutes. Stir in the herbs, season with salt and pepper and pour in the stock. Bring to the boil.

2 Transfer the vegetable mixture to the slow cooker, cover and cook on high for 3 hours until tender. Taste and adjust the seasoning if necessary. Using a slotted spoon, transfer the medley to warmed plates, then spoon over a little of the cooking liquid. Serve immediately.

74

Aubergine Timbales

SERVES 4

2 aubergines

3 tbsp olive oil, plus extra
    for greasing

2 onions, finely chopped

2 red peppers, deseeded
    and chopped

1 large tomato, peeled and chopped

6 tbsp milk

2 egg yolks

pinch of ground cinnamon

85 g/3 oz crispbread, finely crushed

300 ml/10 fl oz soured cream

salt and pepper

fresh flat-leaf parsley sprigs,
    to garnish

Method

1 Halve the aubergines and scoop out the flesh. Reserve the shells and dice the flesh. Heat the oil in a large heavy-based frying pan. Add the onions and cook over a low heat, for 5 minutes. Add the diced aubergines, red peppers and tomato and cook, stirring occasionally, for 15–20 minutes, until all the vegetables are soft. Remove the pan from the heat.

2 Transfer the mixture to a food processor or blender and process to a purée, then scrape into a bowl. Beat the milk, egg yolks and cinnamon in a jug. Season, then stir into the vegetable purée.

3 Brush four ramekins or cups with oil and sprinkle with enough of the crispbread crumbs to coat. Tip out any excess. Mix about three quarters of the remaining crumbs into the vegetable purée. Slice the aubergine shells into strips and use them to line the ramekins, leaving the ends overlapping the rims. Spoon the filling into the ramekins, sprinkle with the remaining crumbs and fold over the overlapping ends of the aubergine. Cover the ramekins with foil.

4 Stand the ramekins on a trivet in the slow cooker and pour in enough boiling water to come about one third of the way up the sides of the ramekins. Cover and cook on high for 2 hours.

5 To make the sauce, lightly beat the soured cream and season. Lift the ramekins out of the slow cooker and remove the foil. Invert onto serving plates, garnish with parsley sprigs and serve immediately with the sauce.

75

Cabbage Roulades

SERVES 6

225 g/8 oz mixed nuts, finely ground

2 onions, finely chopped

1 garlic clove, finely chopped

2 celery sticks, finely chopped

115 g/4 oz Cheddar cheese, grated

1 tsp finely chopped fresh thyme

2 eggs

1 tsp yeast extract

12 large green cabbage leaves

Tomato sauce

2 tbsp sunflower oil

2 onions, chopped

2 garlic cloves, finely chopped

600 g/1 lb 5 oz canned chopped
    tomatoes

2 tbsp tomato purée

1 1/2 tsp sugar

1 bay leaf

salt and pepper

Method

1 To make the tomato sauce, heat the oil in a heavy-based saucepan. Add the onions and cook over a medium heat, stirring occasionally, for 5 minutes, until softened. Stir in the garlic and cook for 1 minute, then add the tomatoes, tomato purée, sugar and bay leaf. Season to taste with salt and pepper and bring to the boil. Reduce the heat and simmer gently for 20 minutes, until thickened.

2 Meanwhile, mix together the nuts, onions, garlic, celery, cheese and thyme in a bowl. Lightly beat the eggs with the yeast extract in a jug, then stir into the nut mixture. Set aside.

3 Cut out the thick stalk from the cabbage leaves. Blanch the leaves in a large saucepan of boiling water for 5 minutes, then drain and refresh under cold water. Pat dry with kitchen paper.

4 Place a little of the nut mixture on the stalk end of each cabbage leaf. Fold the sides over, then roll up to make a neat parcel. Repeat with the remaining leaves and nut mixture.

5 Arrange the parcels in the slow cooker, seam-side down. Remove and discard the bay leaf from the tomato sauce and pour the sauce over the cabbage rolls. Cover and cook on low for 3–4 hours. Serve the cabbage roulades hot or cold.

76

Mixed Vegetable Casserole

SERVES 4

400 g/14 oz canned cannellini beans, drained and rinsed

400 g/14 oz canned artichoke hearts, drained

1 red pepper, deseeded and sliced

4 small turnips, sliced

225 g/8 oz baby spinach leaves, coarse stalks removed

6 fresh thyme sprigs

400 g/14 oz frozen baby broad beans

1 tbsp olive oil

25 g/1 oz butter

4 shallots, chopped

4 leeks, sliced

3 celery sticks, sliced

3 tbsp plain flour

200 ml/7 fl oz dry white wine

150 ml/5 fl oz vegetable stock

salt and pepper

Method

1 Put the cannellini beans, artichoke hearts, red pepper, turnips, spinach and 4 of the thyme sprigs into the slow cooker.

2 Cook the broad beans in a small saucepan of lightly salted boiling water for 10 minutes.

3 Meanwhile, heat the oil and butter in a large frying pan. Add the shallots, leeks and celery and cook over a low heat, stirring occasionally, for 5 minutes, until softened. Stir in the flour and cook, stirring constantly, for 1 minute. Gradually stir in the wine and stock and bring to the boil, stirring constantly. Season to taste with salt and pepper.

4 Transfer the contents of the frying pan to the slow cooker. Drain the broad beans and add to the slow cooker. Stir well, cover and cook on low for 2½–3 hours. Remove and discard the thyme sprigs. Transfer to warmed serving dishes and garnish with the remaining thyme sprigs. Serve immediately.

77

Summer Vegetable Casserole

SERVES 4

500 g/1 lb 2 oz potatoes, peeled
  and cubed

2 courgettes, cubed

2 red peppers, deseeded and cubed

2 red onions, sliced

2 tsp mixed dried herbs

250 ml/9 fl oz hot vegetable stock

salt and pepper

Method

1 Layer all the vegetables in the slow cooker, sprinkling with herbs and salt and pepper between the layers.

2 Pour over the stock. Cover and cook on low for 7 hours. Transfer to warmed serving bowls and serve immediately.

78

Parsley Dumpling Stew

SERVES 6

½ swede, cut into chunks

2 onions, sliced

2 potatoes, cut into chunks

2 carrots, cut into chunks

2 celery sticks, sliced

2 courgettes, sliced

2 tbsp tomato purée

600 ml/1 pint hot vegetable stock

1 bay leaf

1 tsp ground coriander

½ tsp dried thyme

400 g/14 oz canned
   sweetcorn, drained

salt and pepper

Parsley dumplings

200 g/7 oz self-raising flour

pinch of salt

115 g/4 oz vegetable suet

2 tbsp chopped fresh flat-leaf
   parsley, plus extra sprigs
   to garnish

about 125 ml/4 fl oz milk

Method

1 Put the swede, onions, potatoes, carrots, celery and courgettes into the slow cooker. Stir the tomato purée into the stock and pour it over the vegetables. Add the bay leaf, coriander and thyme and season to taste with salt and pepper. Cover and cook on low for 6 hours.

2 To make the dumplings, sift the flour with the salt into a bowl and stir in the suet and chopped parsley. Add just enough of the milk to make a firm but light dough. Knead lightly and shape into 12 small balls.

3 Stir the sweetcorn into the mixture in the slow cooker and place the dumplings on top. Cook on high for 30 minutes. Transfer to warmed serving plates, garnish with parsley sprigs and serve immediately.

79

Spring Stew

SERVES 4

2 tbsp olive oil

4–8 baby onions, halved

2 celery sticks, cut into 5-mm/
 1/4-inch slices

225 g/8 oz young carrots,
 halved if large

300 g/10 1/2 oz new potatoes, halved

850 ml–1.2 litres/1 1/2–2 pints
 vegetable stock

225 g/8 oz dried haricot beans,
 soaked overnight in cold water
 and drained

1 bouquet garni

1 1/2–2 tbsp light soy sauce

85 g/3 oz baby sweetcorn

115 g/4 oz shelled broad beans,
 thawed if frozen

225 g/8 oz Savoy cabbage, shredded

1 1/2 tbsp cornflour

salt and pepper

55–85 g/2–3 oz Parmesan-style
 vegetarian cheese, grated, to serve

Method

1 Heat the oil in a saucepan. Add the onions, celery, carrots and potatoes and cook over a low heat, stirring frequently, for 5–8 minutes until softened. Add the stock, haricot beans, bouquet garni and soy sauce, bring to the boil, then transfer to the slow cooker.

2 Add the sweetcorn, broad beans and cabbage, season with salt and pepper and stir well. Cover and cook on high for 3–4 hours until the vegetables are tender.

3 Remove and discard the bouquet garni. Stir the cornflour and 3 tbsp water to a paste in a small bowl, then stir into the stew. Re-cover and cook on high for a further 15 minutes until thickened. Serve the stew with the cheese.

80

Stuffed Peppers

SERVES 4

100 g/3½ oz basmati rice

4 red peppers

400 g/14 oz can chickpeas, drained

*100 g/3½ oz canned or
    frozen sweetcorn*

4 spring onions, sliced

1 tbsp chopped fresh thyme

1 tbsp olive oil

150 ml/¼ pint vegetable stock

salt and pepper

Method

1 Cook the rice in lightly salted, boiling water for 10 minutes, until almost tender. Drain well.

2 Slice the tops from the peppers and remove the seeds and membranes. Cut a small slice from the base of each so they sit firmly.

3 Mix together the rice, chickpeas, sweetcorn, onions, thyme, oil, salt and pepper. Spoon into the peppers and replace the lids.

4 Place the peppers in the slow cooker. Pour in the stock, cover and cook on low for 5 hours or until tender. Transfer to warmed serving plates and serve immediately.

81

Baked Aubergine with Courgette

SERVES 4

2 large aubergines

olive oil, for brushing

2 large courgettes, sliced

4 tomatoes, sliced

1 garlic clove, finely chopped

15 g/½ oz dry breadcrumbs

15 g/½ oz Parmesan-style
  vegetarian cheese, grated

salt and pepper

basil leaves, to garnish

Method

1 Cut the aubergines into fairly thin slices and brush with oil. Heat a large griddle pan or heavy-based frying pan over a high heat, then add the aubergines and cook in batches for 6–8 minutes, turning once, until soft and brown.

2 Layer the aubergines in the slow cooker with the courgettes, tomatoes and garlic, seasoning with salt and pepper between the layers.

3 Mix the breadcrumbs with the cheese and sprinkle over the vegetables. Cover and cook on low for 4 hours.

4 Transfer to warmed serving bowls, garnish with basil leaves and serve immediately.

82

Sweet & Sour Sicilian Pasta

SERVES 4

4 tbsp olive oil

1 large red onion, sliced

2 garlic cloves, finely chopped

2 red peppers, deseeded and sliced

2 courgettes, cut into batons

1 aubergine, cut into batons

450 ml/16 fl oz passata

4 tbsp lemon juice

2 tbsp balsamic vinegar

55 g/2 oz stoned black olives, sliced

1 tbsp sugar

400 g/14 oz dried fettuccine

salt and pepper

fresh flat-leaf parsley sprigs,
    to garnish

Method

1 Heat the oil in a large, heavy-based saucepan. Add the onion, garlic and peppers and cook over a low heat, stirring occasionally, for 5 minutes. Add the courgettes and aubergine and cook, stirring occasionally, for 5 minutes more. Stir in the passata and 150 ml/5 fl oz water and bring to the boil. Stir in the lemon juice, vinegar, olives and sugar and season with salt and pepper.

2 Transfer the mixture to the slow cooker. Cover and cook on low for 5 hours until all the vegetables are tender.

3 To cook the pasta, bring a large saucepan of lightly salted water to the boil. Add the fettuccine and bring back to the boil. Cook for 10–12 minutes until the pasta is tender but still firm to the bite. Drain and transfer to a warm serving dish. Spoon the vegetable mixture over the pasta, toss lightly, garnish with parsley and serve.

83

Vegetable Pasta

SERVES 4

250 g/9 oz dried penne pasta

2 tbsp olive oil, plus extra
   for drizzling

1 red onion, sliced

2 courgettes, thinly sliced

200 g/7 oz closed cup
   mushrooms, sliced

2 tbsp chopped fresh oregano

300 g/10½ oz tomatoes, sliced

55 g/2 oz Parmesan-style vegetarian
   cheese, grated

salt and pepper

Method

1 Bring a large pan of lightly salted water to the boil. Add the pasta, bring back to the boil and cook for 8–10 minutes, or until tender but still firm to the bite. Drain. Meanwhile, heat the oil in a heavy-based saucepan, add the onions and cook over a medium heat, stirring occasionally, for 5 minutes, until softened. Stir into the pasta.

2 Place a layer of courgettes and mushrooms in the slow cooker and top with a layer of pasta. Sprinkle with oregano, salt and pepper and continue layering, finishing with a layer of vegetables.

3 Arrange the sliced tomatoes on top and drizzle with oil. Cover and cook on high for 3 hours, or until tender.

4 Sprinkle with cheese, cover and cook for a further 10 minutes. Transfer to a warmed serving bowl and serve immediately.

84

Vegetable Curry

SERVES 4-6

2 tbsp vegetable oil

1 tsp cumin seeds

1 onion, sliced

2 curry leaves

2.5-cm/1-inch piece fresh ginger, finely chopped

2 fresh red chillies, deseeded and chopped

2 tbsp Indian curry paste

2 carrots, sliced

115 g/4 oz mangetout

1 cauliflower, cut into florets

3 tomatoes, peeled and chopped

85 g/3 oz frozen peas, thawed

1/2 tsp ground turmeric

150–225 ml/5–8 fl oz hot vegetable stock

salt and pepper

naan breads, to serve

Method

1 Heat the oil in a large heavy-based saucepan. Add the cumin seeds and cook, stirring constantly, for 1–2 minutes, until they give off their aroma and begin to pop. Add the onion and curry leaves and cook, stirring occasionally, for 5 minutes, until the onion has softened. Add the ginger and chillies and cook, stirring occasionally, for 1 minute.

2 Stir in the curry paste and cook, stirring, for 2 minutes, then add the carrots, mangetout and cauliflower. Cook for 5 minutes, then add the tomatoes, peas and turmeric and season to taste with salt and pepper. Cook for 3 minutes, then add 150 ml/5 fl oz of the stock and bring to the boil.

3 Transfer the mixture to the slow cooker. If the vegetables are not covered by the liquid, add more hot stock, then cover and cook on low for 5 hours, until tender. Remove and discard the curry leaves. Transfer to warmed serving dishes and serve immediately with naan breads.

85

Vegetarian Paella

SERVES 6

4 tbsp olive oil

1 Spanish onion, sliced

2 garlic cloves, finely chopped

1 litre/1¾ pints hot vegetable stock

large pinch of saffron threads,
   lightly crushed

1 yellow pepper, deseeded and sliced

1 red pepper, deseeded and sliced

1 large aubergine, diced

225 g/8 oz paella or risotto rice

450 g/1 lb tomatoes, peeled
   and chopped

115 g/4 oz chestnut mushrooms,
   sliced

115 g/4 oz French beans, halved

400 g/14 oz canned borlotti beans,
   drained and rinsed

salt and pepper

Method

1 Heat the oil in a large frying pan. Add the onion and garlic and cook over a low heat, stirring occasionally, for 5 minutes, until softened. Put 3 tablespoons of the hot stock into a small bowl and stir in the saffron, then set aside to infuse.

2 Add the peppers and aubergine to the pan and cook, stirring occasionally, for 5 minutes. Add the rice and cook, stirring constantly, for 1 minute, until the grains are coated with oil and glistening. Pour in the remaining stock and add the tomatoes, mushrooms, French beans and borlotti beans. Stir in the saffron mixture and season to taste with salt and pepper.

3 Transfer the mixture to the slow cooker, cover and cook on low for 2½–3 hours, until the rice is tender and the stock has been absorbed. Transfer to warmed serving plates and serve immediately.

86

Mixed Bean Chilli

SERVES 4–6

2 tbsp corn oil

1 onion, chopped

1 garlic clove, finely chopped

1 fresh red chilli, deseeded and chopped

1 yellow pepper, deseeded and chopped

1 tsp ground cumin

1 tbsp chilli powder

115 g/4 oz dried red kidney beans, soaked overnight, drained and rinsed

115 g/4 oz dried black beans, soaked overnight, drained and rinsed

115 g/4 oz dried pinto beans, soaked overnight, drained and rinsed

1 litre/1¾ pints vegetable stock

1 tbsp sugar

salt and pepper

chopped fresh coriander, to garnish

crusty bread, to serve

Method

1 Heat the oil in a large heavy-based saucepan. Add the onion, garlic, chilli and yellow pepper and cook over a medium heat, stirring occasionally, for 5 minutes. Stir in the cumin and chilli powder and cook, stirring, for 1–2 minutes. Add the drained beans and stock and bring to the boil. Boil vigorously for 15 minutes.

2 Transfer the mixture to the slow cooker, cover and cook on low for 10 hours, until the beans are tender.

3 Season to taste with salt and pepper, then ladle about one third into a bowl. Mash well with a potato masher, then return the mashed beans to the slow cooker and stir in the sugar. Transfer to warmed serving bowls and garnish with chopped coriander. Serve immediately with crusty bread.

87

Spring Vegetable Risotto

SERVES 4

1.2 litres/2 pints vegetable stock

large pinch of saffron threads

55 g/2 oz butter

1 tbsp olive oil

1 onion, chopped

2 garlic cloves, finely chopped

225 g/8 oz risotto rice

3 tbsp dry white wine

1 bay leaf

250 g/9 oz mixed spring vegetables,
such as asparagus spears, French
beans, baby carrots, baby broad
beans and petits pois, thawed
if frozen

2 tbsp chopped flat-leaf parsley

55 g/2 oz Parmesan-style vegetarian
cheese, grated

salt and pepper

Method

1 Put 6 tablespoons of the stock into a small bowl, crumble in the saffron threads and leave to infuse. Reserve 150 ml/5 fl oz of the remaining stock and heat the remainder in a saucepan.

2 Meanwhile, melt half of the butter with the oil in a separate large saucepan. Add the onion and garlic and cook over a low heat, stirring occasionally, for 5 minutes, until softened. Stir in the rice and cook, stirring constantly, for 1–2 minutes, until all the grains are coated and glistening. Pour in the wine and cook, stirring constantly, for a few minutes, until all the alcohol has evaporated. Season to taste with salt and pepper. Pour in the hot stock and the saffron mixture, add the bay leaf and bring to the boil, stirring constantly.

3 Transfer the mixture to the slow cooker, cover and cook on low for 2 hours. Meanwhile, if using fresh vegetables, slice the asparagus spears, French beans and carrots and blanch all the vegetables in boiling water for 5 minutes. Drain and reserve.

4 Stir the reserved stock into the rice mixture, if it seems dry, and add the mixed vegetables, sprinkling them evenly over the top. Re-cover and cook on low for a further 30–45 minutes, until heated through.

5 Remove and discard the bay leaf. Gently stir in the parsley, the remaining butter and the cheese and serve immediately.

88

Asparagus & Spinach Risotto

SERVES 4

2 tbsp olive oil

4 shallots, finely chopped

280 g/10 oz arborio rice

1 garlic clove, crushed

100 ml/3 1/2 fl oz dry white wine

850 ml/1 1/2 pints vegetable stock

200 g/7 oz asparagus spears

200 g/7 oz baby spinach leaves

40 g/1 1/2 oz Parmesan-style
vegetarian cheese, grated

salt and pepper

Method

1 Heat the oil in a frying pan, add the shallots and fry over a medium heat, stirring, for 2–3 minutes. Add the rice and garlic and cook for a further 2 minutes, stirring. Add the wine and allow it to boil for 30 seconds.

2 Transfer the rice mixture to the slow cooker, add the stock and season to taste with salt and pepper. Cover and cook on high for 2 hours, or until most of the liquid is absorbed.

3 Cut the asparagus into 4.5-cm/1 1/2 -inch lengths. Stir into the rice, then spread the spinach over the top. Replace the lid and cook on high for a further 30 minutes, until the asparagus is just tender and the spinach is wilted.

4 Stir in the spinach with the cheese, then adjust the seasoning to taste and serve immediately in warmed bowls.

5

Cakes & Desserts

89

Chocolate Cake

SERVES 8

375 g/13 oz plain dark chocolate

175 g/6 oz unsalted butter,
  plus extra for greasing

175 g/6 oz light muscovado sugar

4 eggs

2 tsp vanilla extract

150 g/5½ oz self-raising flour

55 g/2 oz ground almonds

125 ml/4 fl oz double cream

Method

1 Place a trivet or a ring of crumpled foil in the base of the slow cooker. Grease and base-line a 20-cm/8-inch diameter, deep cake tin, or a tin that fits into your slow cooker.

2 Melt 250 g/9 oz chocolate in a bowl over a pan of hot water. Remove from the heat and cool slightly.

3 Beat the butter and sugar in a large bowl until pale and fluffy. Gradually beat in the eggs. Stir in the melted chocolate and 1 teaspoon vanilla extract. Fold in the flour and almonds evenly.

4 Spoon the mixture into the tin, spreading evenly. Place in the slow cooker, cover and cook on high for 2½ hours or until risen and springy to the touch.

5 Remove from the slow cooker and leave the cake in the tin for 10 minutes. Turn out and cool on a wire rack.

6 Place the remaining chocolate and vanilla extract in a pan with the cream and heat gently, stirring, until melted. Cool until thick enough to spread. Split the cake into two layers and sandwich together with the filling.

90

Chocolate & Walnut Sponge

SERVES 4–6

55 g/2 oz cocoa powder,
  plus extra for dusting

2 tbsp milk

115 g/4 oz self-raising flour

pinch of salt

115 g/4 oz unsalted butter, softened,
  plus extra for greasing

115 g/4 oz caster sugar

2 eggs, lightly beaten

55 g/2 oz walnut halves, chopped

whipped cream, to serve

Method

1 Grease a 1.2-litre/2-pint pudding basin with butter. Cut out a double round of greaseproof paper that is 7 cm/2¾ inches wider than the rim of the basin. Grease one side with butter and make a pleat in the centre.

2 Mix the cocoa and the milk to a paste in a small bowl. Sift the flour and salt into a separate small bowl. Set aside.

3 Beat together the butter and sugar in a large bowl until pale and fluffy. Gradually beat in the eggs, a little at a time, then gently fold in the sifted flour mixture, followed by the cocoa mixture and the walnuts.

4 Spoon the mixture into the prepared basin. Cover the basin with the greaseproof paper rounds, buttered-side down, and tie in place with string. Stand the basin on a trivet in the slow cooker and pour in enough boiling water to come about halfway up the side of the basin. Cover and cook on high for 3–3½ hours.

5 Carefully remove the basin from the slow cooker and discard the greaseproof paper. Run a knife around the inside of the basin, then turn out onto a warmed serving dish. Serve immediately with whipped cream, dusted with cocoa.

91

Hazelnut Steamed Sponge

SERVES 6

115 g/4 oz toasted hazelnuts, chopped

115 g/4 oz unsalted butter, plus extra for greasing

115 g/4 oz soft dark brown sugar

2 eggs, lightly beaten

115 g/4 oz self-raising flour

1 tbsp lemon juice

Toffee sauce

55 g/2 oz unsalted butter

55 g/2 oz soft dark brown sugar

4 tbsp double cream

1 tbsp lemon juice

Method

1 Grease an 850-ml/1½-pint pudding basin with butter and sprinkle half the nuts over the base. Cut out a double round of greaseproof paper that is 7 cm/2¾ inches wider than the rim of the basin. Make a pleat in the centre.

2 To make the toffee sauce, put the butter, sugar, cream and lemon juice into a saucepan. Set the pan over a very low heat and stir until the mixture is smooth and thoroughly combined. Remove the pan from the heat. Pour half the sauce into the prepared basin and swirl gently to coat part of the side. Reserve the remainder.

3 Beat together the butter and sugar in a bowl until light and fluffy. Gradually beat in the eggs, then gently fold in the flour, lemon juice and the remaining hazelnuts. Spoon the mixture into the basin. Cover the basin with the greaseproof paper rounds and tie in place with string.

4 Stand the basin on a trivet in the slow cooker and pour in enough boiling water to come about halfway up the side of the basin. Cover and cook on high for 3–3¼ hours, until just set.

5 Shortly before serving, gently reheat the reserved toffee sauce. Carefully remove the basin from the slow cooker and discard the greaseproof paper. Run a knife around the inside of the basin, then turn out onto a warmed serving dish. Serve with the reserved toffee sauce.

92

Lemon Sponge

SERVES 4

140 g/5 oz caster sugar
3 eggs, separated
300 ml/10 fl oz milk
3 tbsp self-raising flour, sifted
150 ml/5 fl oz lemon juice
icing sugar, for dusting

Method

1 Using an electric mixer, beat the caster sugar with the egg yolks in a bowl. Gradually beat in the milk, followed by the flour and the lemon juice.

2 Whisk the egg whites in a separate grease-free bowl until stiff. Fold half the whites into the yolk mixture using a plastic spatula in a figure-of-eight movement, then fold in the remainder. Try not to knock out the air.

3 Pour the mixture into a heatproof dish and cover with foil. Stand the dish on a trivet in the slow cooker and pour in enough boiling water to come about one third of the way up the side of the dish. Cover and cook on high for 2½ hours, until the mixture has set and the sauce and sponge have separated.

4 Carefully remove the dish from the slow cooker and discard the foil. Transfer to warmed bowls, lightly dust with icing sugar and serve immediately.

93

Strawberry Cheesecake

SERVES 6–8

85 g/3 oz unsalted butter, melted

140 g/5 oz digestive biscuits, crushed

300 g/10½ oz strawberries

600 g/1 lb 5 oz full fat soft cheese

225 g/8 oz caster sugar

2 large eggs, beaten

2 tbsp cornflour

finely grated rind and juice of 1 lemon

Method

1 Place a trivet or a ring of crumpled foil in the base of the slow cooker. Stir the butter into the crushed biscuits and press into the base of a 20-cm/8-inch round springform tin, or a tin that fits into your slow cooker.

2 Purée or mash half the strawberries and whisk together with the cheese, sugar, eggs, cornflour, lemon rind and juice until smooth.

3 Tip the mixture into the tin and place in the slow cooker. Cover and cook on high for about 2 hours or until almost set.

4 Turn off the slow cooker and leave the cheesecake in the cooker for 2 hours. Remove and cool completely, then carefully turn out of the tin.

5 Decorate with the remaining strawberries and serve.

94

Apple Crumble

SERVES 4

55 g/2 oz plain flour

55 g/2 oz rolled oats

150 g/5½ oz light muscovado sugar

½ tsp freshly grated nutmeg

½ tsp ground cinnamon

115 g/4 oz unsalted butter, softened

*4 cooking apples, peeled,
   cored and sliced*

4–5 tbsp apple juice

Greek yogurt, to serve

Method

1 Sift the flour into a bowl and stir in the oats, sugar, nutmeg and cinnamon. Add the butter and mix in with a pastry blender or the tines of a fork.

2 Place the apple slices in the base of the slow cooker and add the apple juice. Sprinkle the flour mixture evenly over them.

3 Cover and cook on low for 5½ hours. Serve hot, warm or cold with yogurt.

95

Rice Pudding

SERVES 4

140 g/5 oz short-grain rice

1 litre/1¾ pints milk

115 g/4 oz granulated sugar

1 tsp vanilla extract

ground cinnamon,
*   to decorate*

Method

1 Rinse the rice well under cold running water and drain thoroughly. Pour the milk into a large heavy-based saucepan, add the sugar and bring to the boil, stirring constantly. Sprinkle in the rice, stir well and simmer gently for 10–15 minutes. Transfer the mixture to a heatproof dish and cover with foil.

2 Stand the dish on a trivet in the slow cooker and pour in enough boiling water to come about one third of the way up the side of the dish. Cover and cook on high for 2 hours.

3 Remove the dish from the slow cooker and discard the foil. Stir the vanilla extract into the rice, then spoon it into warmed bowls. Lightly dust with cinnamon and serve immediately.

96

Italian Bread Pudding

SERVES 6

unsalted butter, for greasing

6 slices panettone

3 tbsp Marsala

300 ml/10 fl oz milk

300 ml/10 fl oz single cream

100 g/3½ oz caster sugar

grated rind of ½ lemon

pinch of ground cinnamon

3 large eggs, lightly beaten

Method

1 Grease a 1-litre/1¾ -pint pudding basin with butter. Place the panettone on a deep plate and sprinkle with the Marsala.

2 Pour the milk and cream into a pan and add the sugar, lemon rind and cinnamon. Gradually bring to the boil over a low heat, stirring until the sugar has dissolved. Remove the pan from the heat and leave to cool slightly, then pour the mixture onto the eggs, beating constantly.

3 Place the panettone in the prepared basin, pour in the egg mixture and cover with foil. Stand the basin on a trivet in the slow cooker and pour in enough boiling water to come about one third of the way up the side of the basin. Cover and cook on high for 2½ hours, until set.

4 Carefully remove the basin from the slow cooker and discard the foil. Leave to cool, then chill in the refrigerator until required. Run a knife around the inside of the basin, then turn out onto a serving dish. Serve immediately.

97

Thai Black Rice Pudding

SERVES 4

175 g/6 oz black glutinous rice

2 tbsp soft light brown sugar

450 ml/16 fl oz canned coconut milk

225 ml/8 fl oz water

3 eggs

2 tbsp caster sugar

Method

1 Mix together the rice, brown sugar and half the coconut milk in a saucepan, then stir in the water. Bring to the boil, then reduce the heat and simmer, stirring occasionally, for 15 minutes, until almost all the liquid has been absorbed. Transfer the mixture to a heatproof dish or individual ramekins.

2 Lightly beat the eggs with the remaining coconut milk and the caster sugar. Strain, then pour the mixture over the rice.

3 Cover the dish with foil. Stand the dish on a trivet in the slow cooker and pour in enough boiling water to come about one third of the way up the side of the dish. Cover and cook on high for 2–2½ hours, until set. Carefully remove the dish from the slow cooker and discard the foil. Serve hot or cold.

98

Almond Charlotte

SERVES 4

unsalted butter, for greasing

10–12 sponge fingers

300 ml/10 fl oz milk

2 eggs

2 tbsp caster sugar

55 g/2 oz blanched almonds, chopped

4–5 drops almond extract

Sherry sauce

1 tbsp caster sugar

3 egg yolks

150 ml/5 fl oz cream sherry

Method

1 Grease a 600-ml/1-pint pudding basin with butter. Line the basin with the sponge fingers, cutting them to fit and placing them cut-sides down and sugar-coated sides outwards. Cover the base of the basin with some of the offcuts.

2 Pour the milk into a saucepan and bring just to the boil, then remove from the heat. Beat together the eggs and sugar in a heatproof bowl until combined, then stir in the milk. Stir in the almonds and almond extract.

3 Carefully pour the mixture into the prepared basin, making sure that the sponge fingers stay in place, and cover with foil. Stand the basin on a trivet in the slow cooker and pour in enough boiling water to come about halfway up the side of the dish. Cover and cook on high for 3–3½ hours, until set.

4 Shortly before serving, make the sherry sauce. Put the sugar, egg yolks and sherry into a heatproof bowl. Set the bowl over a pan of simmering water, without allowing the bottom of the bowl to touch the surface of the water. Whisk well until the mixture thickens, but do not allow it to boil. Remove from the heat.

5 Carefully remove the basin from the slow cooker and discard the foil. Leave to stand for 2–3 minutes, then turn out onto a warmed serving plate. Pour the sherry sauce around it and serve immediately.

99

Crème Brûlée

SERVES 6

1 vanilla pod

1 litre/1¾ pints double cream

6 egg yolks

100 g/3½ oz caster sugar

85 g/3 oz soft light brown sugar

Method

1 Using a sharp knife, split the vanilla pod in half lengthways, scrape the seeds into a saucepan and add the pod. Pour in the cream and bring just to the boil, stirring constantly. Remove from the heat, cover and leave to infuse for 20 minutes.

2 Whisk together the egg yolks and caster sugar in a bowl until thoroughly mixed. Remove and discard the vanilla pod, then whisk the cream into the egg yolk mixture. Strain the mixture into a large jug.

3 Divide the mixture between six ramekins and cover each with foil. Stand the ramekins on a trivet in the slow cooker and pour in enough boiling water to come about halfway up the sides of the ramekins. Cover and cook on low for 3–3½ hours, until just set. Remove the slow cooker pot from the base and leave to cool completely, then remove the ramekins and chill in the refrigerator for at least 4 hours.

4 Preheat the grill. Sprinkle the brown sugar evenly over the surface of each dessert, then cook under the preheated grill for 30–60 seconds, until the sugar has melted and caramelized. Alternatively, you can use a cook's blowtorch. Return the ramekins to the refrigerator and chill for a further hour before serving.

100

Chocolate Pots

SERVES 6

300 ml/10 fl oz single cream

300 ml/10 fl oz milk

225 g/8 oz plain chocolate,
  broken into small pieces

1 large egg

4 egg yolks

4 tbsp caster sugar

150 ml/5 fl oz double cream

chocolate curls, to decorate

Method

1 Pour the single cream and milk into a saucepan and add the chocolate. Set the pan over a very low heat and stir until the chocolate has melted and the mixture is smooth. Remove from the heat and leave to cool for 10 minutes.

2 Beat together the egg, egg yolks and sugar in a bowl until combined. Gradually stir in the chocolate mixture until thoroughly blended, then strain into a jug.

3 Divide the mixture between six ramekins and cover each with foil. Stand the ramekins on a trivet in the slow cooker and pour in enough boiling water to come about halfway up the sides of the ramekins. Cover and cook on low for 3–3 1/2 hours, until just set. Remove the slow cooker pot from the base and leave to cool completely, then remove the ramekins and chill in the refrigerator for at least 4 hours.

4 Whip the double cream in a bowl until it holds soft peaks. Top each chocolate pot with a little of the whipped cream and decorate with chocolate curls. Serve immediately.

Index